The Selcoth Burn heading for the Moffat Water under Croft Head

OFFICIAL GUIDE

The Southern Upland Way

KEN ANDREW

EASTERN SECTION

COUNTRYSIDE COMMISSION FOR SCOTLAND

HMSO

© Crown Copyright 1984
First published 1984

Inside front cover
Traquair House (Scottish Tourist Board)

Inside back cover
Galashiels (Scottish Tourist Board)

Frontispiece
Croft Head and the col to the Wamphray Water from the route above
the Selcoth Burn

Designed by HMSO Graphic Design, Edinburgh

Photographs by Ken Andrew

Cover and map illustrations by Bill Forbes

Front Cover
Cove Harbour

Back Cover
Craigmichen Scar and Croft Head

Map Cover
Melrose Abbey and the Eildon Hills

ISBN 0 11 492363 9

Contents

Foreword

Foreword by Michael Ancram, MP, Minister for Home Affairs and the Environment at the Scottish Office.

The Southern Uplands, from Galloway to the Borders, represent for many people the 'undiscovered' face of Scotland. Yet this is an area rich in fine scenery, steeped in Scottish history and immortalised in our literature. I have been fortunate to have known many of these hills, lochs and valleys all my life and I believe that the opening of the Southern Upland Way long-distance footpath, running for 212 miles from Portpatrick on the south-west coast to Cockburnspath on the eastern seaboard, will bring great pleasure to many walkers, including our visitors from other countries.

This is the first east-west coast-to-coast long-distance footpath to have been officially designated in Britain and I have no doubt that it will stand comparison with Scotland's first long-distance route, the West Highland Way. The Southern Upland Way is, however, of quite distinct character, as well as being more than twice the length of the West Highland Way. The negotiation and development of this fine route has been completed in the remarkably short period of only five years, thanks to the enthusiasm of the planning authorities and the helpful attitude of the many landowners and tenants, farmers and foresters, who were involved.

This guide is a handsome and very readable companion for the walker and its maps are an essential aid for route-finding along the Way. I am therefore very pleased to introduce this publication, which will contribute a great deal to increased enjoyment – and increased understanding – of the Southern Uplands of Scotland.

Michael Ancram

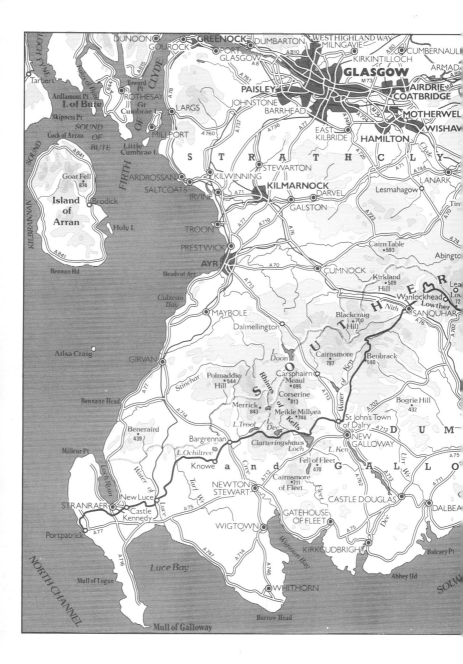

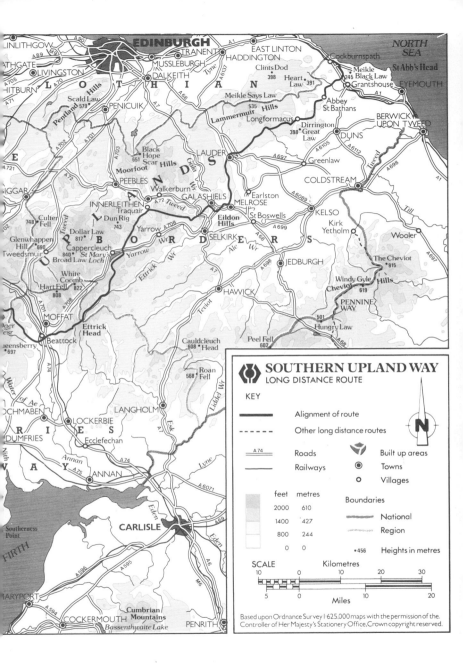

SOUTHERN UPLAND WAY
LONG DISTANCE ROUTE

KEY

———	Alignment of route
- - - - -	Other long distance routes
A74 ———	Roads
———	Railways

	Built up areas
◉	Towns
○	Villages

feet	metres		Boundaries
2000	610		
1400	427		⚬⚬⚬ National
800	244		⚬⚬⚬ Region
0	0		•456 Heights in metres

SCALE   Kilometres

10   0   10   20   30

5   0   10   20
Miles

Based upon Ordnance Survey 1·625,000 maps with the permission of the.
Controller of Her Majesty's Stationery Office, Crown copyright reserved.

9

St Mary's Loch

Introduction

The Southern Upland Way is Britain's first official east-west coast-to-coast long-distance footpath. It is the third Scottish long-distance route to be promoted by the Countryside Commission for Scotland and the first in southern Scotland – although a short stretch of the Pennine Way extends into south Scotland, with its terminus at Kirk Yetholm in the Borders.

Under the Countryside (Scotland) Act 1967, the Countryside Commission for Scotland is given responsibility for preparing and submitting reports to the Secretary of State for Scotland on the development of long-distance routes where it considers that the public should be enabled to make extensive cross-country journeys on foot, avoiding public roads wherever possible. The very popular 152km (95 miles) West Highland Way between Milngavie and Fort William, opened in 1980, and the 96km (60 miles) Speyside Way between Spey Bay on the Moray Firth and Glenmore near Aviemore (the latter as yet only open along part of its length) are both in the Highlands of Scotland.

On 13 July 1979, the Secretary of State for Scotland gave his approval to the Commission's proposals for the Southern Upland Way, running some 340km (212 miles) from Portpatrick on the south-west coast of Scotland – to Cockburnspath on the eastern seaboard. The Southern Upland Way passes through three of Scotland's local authority regions – Dumfries and Galloway, Strathclyde, and Borders. The work of implementing the route, the access negotiations with the many proprietors, and the provision of bridges, stiles, waymarkers and information boards, has been undertaken by these Regional Councils in a remarkably short period of time. It says much for their energy and enthusiasm – and the work of Royal Engineer units of the Army, Scottish Conservation Projects volunteers and local contractors, together with Manpower Services Commission funded

Community Enterprise Project teams – that the route is now available for the use and enjoyment of walkers. Much of the route of the Southern Upland Way follows existing paths and tracks – some of them of ancient origin. Particular thought has been given to the safety of walkers, the interests of wildlife and conservation, and the existing land-uses of farming, forestry and sport. The Way incorporates coastal cliff-top paths, old drove roads and coffin roads, former military roads, forest and farm roads, river and lochside paths, disused railway routes, hill ridges, moorland trails, industrial trails, Roman roads, ecclesiastical roads, coaching roads and – where no route previously existed – it has made its own. The route passes over high hilltops, through deep valleys and across wide moors; it enters towns and villages, crosses trunk roads and railway lines, traverses forests, grouse moors, arable farms and sheep and cattle country. Some stretches of the Way – such as the south side of Glen Trool and the Minchmuir – have been popular leisure-walking routes for generations, whilst the Border Walkway, from Galashiels to Moffat, is a modern concept which has been adopted to the benefit of all. The Southern Upland Way has thus unified a great variety of routes, both ancient and modern, into a noble and mighty idea, providing for walkers a healthy, enjoyable and challenging experience.

As with other long-distance footpaths, the Southern Upland Way will have its critics who will seize on imperfections in the route, and in this Guide. Those critics may suggest that many long-distance walkers are potential vandals, litter-louts and a menace to themselves and to others. Walkers will therefore have the responsibility of proving the critics wrong by using commonsense, courtesy and consideration during their trek across Scotland. No-one would claim that a new footpath over 200 miles in length can be established and used without some adverse effects. What can safely be asserted is that the Southern Upland Way offers a great new opportunity to many walkers. It will introduce many people to exciting new places, and will also help to provide a small, but welcome, boost to the tourist economy of southern Scotland.

There is, strictly speaking, no such thing on the British mainland as a truly natural wilderness. Man's influence is evident in every landscape – even in the renowned Highlands. As in the Highlands, armies have marched and counter-marched over the Southern Uplands, and countless numbers of sheep and cattle have been herded across these hills and through the valleys to the southern markets. Over the centuries these human activities, along with agricultural, sporting and forestry developments, have had a profound effect on the countryside – but the hills are still standing, the lochs are still there and the rivers still flow. Given proper use and wise management, the land will also survive the feet of today's leisure-walkers. In looking at recreational developments of this kind, we have to consider all the influences at work: geology, climate, population changes, social customs, political history, varying patterns of land-use – and the effects of industry. The story of a country's landscape is a complex fabric, woven from many strands. The life and history of Scotland in its many facets, tragic and heroic, is written along the length of the Southern Upland Way, demonstrating a cultural heritage of incredibly rich dimensions. Those who walk this route in its entirety will enjoy a unique educational experience – as well as becoming members of an elite group who can reflect on the sense of physical achievement – and spiritual uplift – which comes from having crossed Scotland from coast to coast on their own two feet.

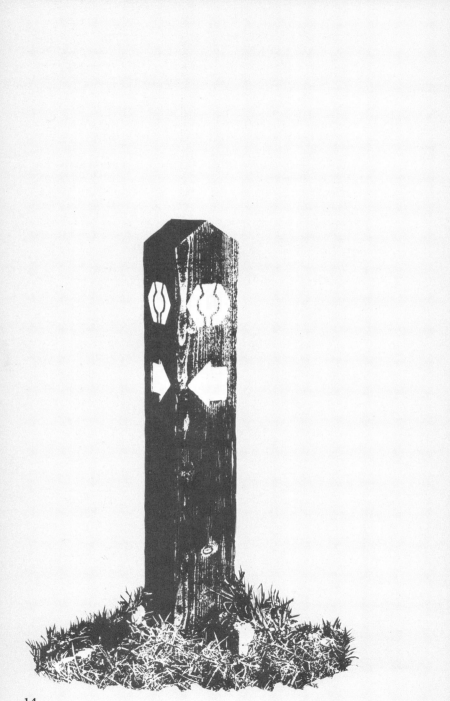

Walking the Way

A 340km (212 miles) walk is not easy – and it must be stressed at the outset that the Southern Upland Way traverses some particularly hard and gruelling stretches of countryside. The West Highland Way and the Speyside Way, in common with many other classic walking routes in Scotland, tend to follow the valleys and lines of least resistance in the landscape. By contrast, the Southern Upland Way, in addition to being more than twice the length of the West Highland Way, has to work its passage *across* the valleys. A study of a map of Scotland will make this clear. The north to south tendency of rivers, roads and railways is more pronounced in the Southern Uplands than elsewhere. Whilst many miles of the Southern Upland Way are on the level, on tarred roads or good footpaths and tracks, many miles are also up and downhill, often through rough vegetation and over generally soft ground. Let no-one be under the misapprehension that, because this walk is set outside the Highlands of Scotland, it can be treated lightly. Those who intend to walk the entire route in one expedition must be very fit and have considerable hillwalking experience. Those who lack this fitness and experience should tackle the route in easier stages. Since the Southern Upland Way crosses the grain of the country, it frequently leaves the valleys and lines of communication behind, threading its way through areas where population is sparse and transport and shelter practically non-existent. For these reasons, walkers who come to the Way ill-equipped cannot simply opt out when the going gets tough. Make no mistake about it, this is a big route in more ways than one.

Direction
This guide, published in two volumes, describes the Way from west to east – and walkers are strongly advised to tackle the route in this direction if they possibly can – starting at Portpatrick and finishing at Cockburnspath. Walking north-

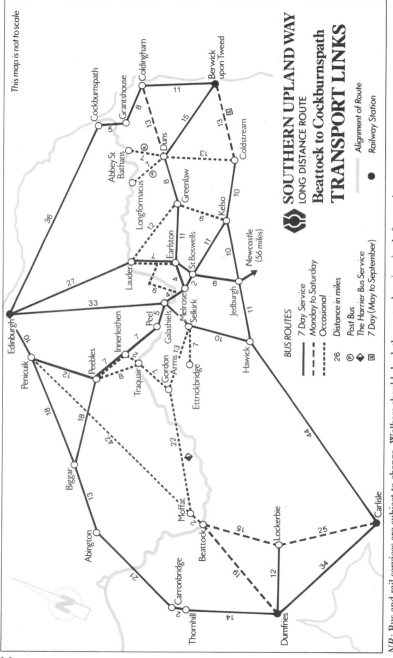

SOUTHERN UPLAND WAY
LONG DISTANCE ROUTE

Beattock to Cockburnspath
TRANSPORT LINKS

This map is not to scale

BUS ROUTES
7 Day Service
Monday to Saturday
Occasional
26   Distance in miles
℗   Post Bus
◆   The Harrier Bus Service
☒   7 Day (May to September)

— Alignment of Route
●   Railway Station

NB: Bus and rail services are subject to change. Walkers should check the up-to-date situation before setting out.

eastwards, the sun is generally at your back and the colour and details of the landscape are more easily seen to the front. The prevailing winds are south-westerly so it is as well to have the weather behind you, too. Walkers tackling the route from east to west will find the accompanying route map provides the best way of navigating the Way in the reverse direction to the guide description.

Weather

Southern Upland weather comes mainly from the Atlantic Ocean. The prevailing westerly winds which affect Scotland are generally very moist after journeying across thousands of miles of sea. Cloudy conditions, grey skies and rain are common – but beautiful spells of sunshine, giving sparkling landscapes, can occur between the fronts and are not so rare as many people may imagine. However, settled conditions rarely last for long, so good judgement is required in choosing the ideal time to tackle the Southern Upland Way! The walker is likely to experience an interesting mix of wind, rain and sunshine on a complete traverse of the Way – although extended periods of settled weather could turn up, giving either a heatwave, unremitting gloom and rain or – ideally – cool, clear and fresh conditions. Rainfall varies across the country, according to height and distance from the coast. From an annual average of about 1000mm (40 inches) at Portpatrick, the average rainfall rises to about 2000mm at Glen Trool and tails off gradually beyond the Lowthers to under 1000mm in the Lammermuirs, down to about 750mm at Cockburnspath. On the lee side of the hills, the east tends to get much less cloud and more sun than the west, but when the wind is from an easterly quarter, the position is reversed. The increasing risk of rain and cloud which comes with altitude should always be borne in mind. It can be a fine day in the valleys or on the coasts, whilst on the hills it is wet and cloudy. The east coast tends to suffer from haar – sea mist – at times and these conditions can prevail on days when it is warm and sunny inland.

February to June can be very dry months, when great care needs to be taken against causing fires, especially in the vicinity of forests and grasslands. July and August may be disappointingly cloudy or hazy, whilst the November to January period tends to be wet and – of course – dark. The risk of being caught out in the dark is something the winter walker needs to guard against. The light can be fading by very early afternoon on a misty hill in mid-winter and, given the substantial distances involved in walking the Southern Upland Way, careful planning is required. No hard and fast rules can be laid down and no guarantees can be given for Southern Upland weather. Generally, however, late spring and early summer are the best periods, with long hours of daylight, reasonable temperatures, fresh growth to brighten the countryside, few midges about, the bracken yet to uncoil above head-height, the shepherd's anxieties over his lambs have lessened, and the vegetation and paths are drying out and allowing faster walking progress.

Novice walkers are safer to confine their outings to the summer months, taking the risk that it could still be cloudy – or unpleasantly hot and muggy with attendant hordes of tormenting insects – for which a repellent is necessary. Heatstroke is another risk and headgear of some kind should be carried in summer. Bare flesh should not be toasted in the sun for too long unless it is used to it, and extra clothes should be carried to replace shorts – and cover up white legs which are beginning to feel the heat. Each season has its own pleasures and miseries and the fit and experienced walker who is not afraid of bouts of rough weather and some discomfort can enjoy the more transient but colourful days, the short-lived autumn colours, the winter frosts and snows, the rainbows and cloudscapes.

The walker by now will have gathered that the weather is the crucial factor on the Southern Upland Way! Enjoyment and success go with good weather so try to get your weather right by studying the forecasts. Satellite pictures on TV are useful in showing the approach of broken skies and clear weather to the British Isles, and TV weather maps can give an idea of what to expect. The most useful radio forecasts are probably those at the start and end of the day on BBC Radio 4 at 12.10am, 6am, 6.55am and 7.55am – or at 6.55am on Radio 3. The shipping forecasts at 12.15am and 6.25am on Radio 4 are also very useful, giving reports of existing weather at various stations around Britain, with the Southern Uplands likely to catch similar conditions downwind within a day. Particular attention should be paid to the shipping forecasts for the areas Irish Sea and Malin – which lie off Galloway, and Forth and Tyne.

Up-to-the-minute forecasts can be obtained by telephoning the Meteorological Offices at Edinburgh Airport, the Glasgow Weather Centre, Prestwick, Newcastle or Pitreavie. The numbers will be found at the start of the telephone directory. This is an excellent service which can provide a forecast tailor-made for any walker.

Following the Way

This guide has been written in two parts, Volume I covering the western section of the route, and Volume II, the east. Each volume has its accompanying route map of four sections. Map section four of Vol. I overlaps with map section one of Vol. II. Walkers planning to undertake the whole length – or large sections of the Way – therefore need both Volumes. Vol. I (West) covers the Way from Portpatrick to Beattock and Vol. II (East) leads on from Beattock to Cockburnspath.

In addition to the two sets of maps and the two volumes of the official guide, walkers also have the assistance of signposts and waymarkers. The dark brown posts carry a thistle within a hexagon symbol, which is the standard identification for a designated long-distance footpath in Scotland. These have been placed at strategic points along the Way to indicate changes of direction, and to confirm that the walker is on the correct line where the route is not obvious. The waymarkers have been erected by the regional planning authorities, who have tried to keep them to a minimum consistent with safety.

Yellow arrows are painted on the waymark posts to show direction whilst the taller signposts are situated at junctions or where the route leaves a road and extra guidance is needed. Remember, waymarkers are a fair-weather aid. The ability to navigate with map and compass is essential: in bad visibility you won't see the markers! Walkers not able to navigate accurately in mist should not attempt the long stretches of hill country on the Way. Stiles and wooden bridges of a standard pattern can also be recognised as route-markers in some places – and where markers are absent, walkers can expect to follow the obvious route, be it a stone wall, fence, forest road or path, until the next waymarker post is seen.

The route maps designed for the Southern Upland Way are crucial for navigation. These have been specially prepared by the Ordnance Survey from its 1:50,000 series. Because of the south-west to north-east alignment of the Way, seven standard OS maps would normally have had to be purchased to provide coverage for this route. To keep bulk and weight to a minimum, the four route map sections accompanying each of the two volumes of the guide show the Way within a relatively narrow corridor. The difficulty of mapping this trans-Scotland footpath has necessitated the maps being skewed at 30°. This puts the north to south grid lines at an angle to the edges of the map sheets – but compass bearings are still taken in relation to the grid lines, despite their unorthodox appearance. It is worth repeating that walkers should have a good knowledge of how to use the map and compass before tackling the entire route – or the remoter stretches of it.

Times and Distances
It is not possible to give a useful estimate of how long a complete traverse of the Southern Upland Way will take. Individual walkers travel at their own speed – and performance will vary considerably, depending upon weather and underfoot conditions. In cool, dry conditions, walkers will romp along much faster than in hot, humid weather – or when the ground is wet. Walking in shirts and shorts will generally be quicker than in rainwear. Navigation in mist can be a slow business, whilst advancing into a headwind is rather more difficult than being bowled along by a tailwind! Rain, wind, sleet or snow – as well as causing discomfort – will hinder access to rucksacks and pockets and make if difficult to use maps and guides. A few walkers may see the Way as some kind of race to be run against the clock or the calendar. It would be wiser not to do so. The normal walker can expect to spend somewhere between 10 and 20 days on the route, depending on fitness.

The guide divides the Way into 15 distinct stretches – seven in the western half (Volume I) and eight in the east (Volume II). These stretches are, however, of unequal length and difficulty. A number of the sections can be done easily by a family party inside a day – but several are very long – the longest being 43km (27 miles) – and very demanding. Sensible walkers will allow two days for these lengthy stretches.

Naismith's Rule can be used to work out a very rough estimate for time and distance. This suggests allowing one hour for every 5km (3 miles) to be walked, plus half-an-hour for every 300m (1000 feet) to be climbed. Circumstances and weather can play havoc with this estimate, of course, and walkers are cautioned to allow themselves plenty of extra time.

Accommodation and Facilities along the Way
A good night's rest is a vital element in achieving a successful day's walking. Most Southern Upland Way walkers will need to find between 10 and 20 different overnight resting places between the west and east coasts. Inevitably, there is a good choice in some localities – and a dearth of facilities in others. The situation will always be subject to alteration and the pages of this guide can therefore give only a general indication of the location and types of accommodation available, together with outline details of other services and facilities

Accommodation and Facilities along the Way: Beattock—Cockburnspath

	information	accommodation	camp site	youth hostel	bothy	snacks/meals	toilets	shops	telephone
Beattock		●	●			●		●	●
(Moffat)	●	●	●			●	●	●	●
Barnhill		●							
Ettrick Head									
(Over Phawhope)					●				
Ettrick Valley		●	●					●	
St Mary's Loch		●	●			●	●	●	●
Yarrow Crossroads									
(Gordon Arms)		●				●			
Traquair						●			●
(Innerleithen)		●	●			●	●	●	●
(Broadmeadows)				●					
(Clovenfords)		●				●			●
(Selkirk)	●	●	●			●	●	●	●
Galashiels	●	●	●			●	●	●	●
Melrose	●	●	●	●		●	●	●	●
Lauder		●	●			●	●	●	●
Wanton Walls		●							
Longformacus		●						●	●
(Duns)		●				●	●	●	●
Abbey St Bathans		●*				●	●		●
Pease Bay								●	
Cove								●	
Cockburnspath		●	●			●	●	●	●
(Coldingham)				●					

* Hostel-type accommodation is planned.
  Settlements shown in brackets are off the route.

important to walkers. A Southern Upland Way accommodation list is issued free by the Countryside Commission for Scotland, from which the up-to-date position can more readily be checked. Copies are available from the Commission on request (address on inside back page) or at local tourist information centres. Additional guidance on holiday accommodation can be obtained from the Scottish Tourist Board, 23 Ravelston Terrace, Edinburgh EH4 3EU or at local tourist information centres. The Board publishes a range of useful accommodation guides. Many places close down in the winter months and many will be fully booked in the high summer. Walkers will save themselves a lot of trouble – and extra walking – if they seek and plan their accommodation in advance through tourist information centres. Registers will be kept of some of the beds available in the locality – and in many cases staff may be able to make a telephone booking, saving walkers the torment of walking around town and country looking at 'No Vacancies' signs. For current information, contact: Dumfries and Galloway Tourist Board, Douglas House, Newton Stewart (Tel: 0671 2549) and Scottish Borders Tourist Board, Municipal Buildings, High Street, Selkirk (Tel: 0750 20555).

Youth Hostels

There are six youth hostels which could be of use to Southern Upland Way walkers. They are provided by the Scottish Youth Hostels Association and are available only to members of that Association. However, walkers can join the SYHA at any of the hostels by paying a modest enrolment fee. Overnight charges are also very modest, varying according to the member's age and the grade of the hostel. The hostels on or near the way are:

Portpatrick—Beattock

Minnigaff (Newton Stewart) (GR 411663): Grade 3, 44 beds, 25 March-1 October.

Kendoon (GR 616883): Grade 3, 38 beds, 15 May-1 October, also Friday, Saturday and Sunday at Easter, and Saturdays from Easter to 15 May.

Wanlockhead (GR 874131): Grade 3, 30 beds, 25 March-1 October and Saturdays in winter.

Beattock—Cockburnspath

Broadmeadows (GR 417303): Grade 3, 28 beds, 25 March-1 October.

Melrose (GR 550340): Grade 2, 90 beds, 9 March-30 October. Friday and Saturday in winter and normally at New Year. Closed during November.

Coldingham (GR 915664): Grade 2, 68 beds, 25 March-1 October.

Hostels are generally busiest at the weekends and in the summer months and during Easter holidays. Bookings can be made in advance to ensure admittance. For details of membership and a current handbook, write to: Secretary, SYHA, 7 Glebe Crescent, Stirling FK8 2JA.

Bothies

The White Laggan (GR 466775) at Loch Dee – and Over Phawhope (GR 182082) north-east of Ettrick Head – are simple, unlocked bothies providing wind and watertight shelter, but lacking in facilities. These bothies are available for use by walkers but they could be crowded at times.

Camping

Many Way walkers will be campers and backpackers and a waterproof tent with fly-sheet and sewn-in groundsheet is strongly recommended. Campers should use recognised camp sites where these are available along the Way. Campers should always seek permission before pitching their tents and random camping is specifically prohibited in some areas, for example in the Galloway Forest Park, except at the Forestry Commission's Caldons Camp Site. Avoid camping anywhere near plantations; where stock are grazing, or in the vicinity of grouse moors. Attitudes to campers – who could represent a large proportion of all Way walkers – will be determined by the behaviour of the campers themselves and courtesy, tidiness and consideration for others are more likely to lead to a welcome than are thoughtless behaviour and leaving litter behind. Campers will have a special responsibility in ensuring a welcome for those walkers who come after them.

Transport

Public transport in the Southern Uplands normally involves buses. The Way crosses or passes close to a number of bus routes, which will allow walkers to join or leave the Way. The south of Scotland is thinly populated and buses are infrequent – and may be non-existent in some areas. A map showing the main transport links will be found on page 16. The Portpatrick-Beattock section of the Way is served by Western Scottish bus services and the Beattock-Cockburnspath section by Eastern Scottish. Additional services are provided by local operators such as J. & J. Leith Ltd, Sanquhar, and Creightons of Moffat. Post buses carrying mail – and a very limited number of passengers – operate at New Luce, Longformacus and Abbey St Bathans. Railways remaining in the Southern Uplands either tend to skirt round the periphery of the Way – or hurtle non-stop across it. Few railway stations exist anywhere near the Way. Bus and rail timetables are subject to regular revision so it is advisable to check in advance. Details of main bus services can be obtained from the Travel Centre, Buchanan Bus Station, Killermont Street, Glasgow G2 3NP. Timetables for other services may be obtained at tourist information centres.

Clothing and Equipment

Allowing for a fortnight's walking – much of it in the hills – requires a good deal of thought to be given to the safe minimum amount of equipment required. The more weight you carry, the slower is your progress – and the longer you take for the journey. Thus you need extra clothing and equipment! It is a vicious circle. Work out what is the minimum amount of gear you need, allowing for season and probable weather, and then add a margin for error and unforeseen setbacks. Good quality hill-walking kit is essential for those tackling any substantial part of the route, or even one section in cold, wet or changeable weather conditions. You *might* survive in shorts and sandshoes over some parts of the route in summer, if you are lucky with the weather, but it would be foolish to attempt to do so without having reserves of warm and waterproof clothing in your rucksack. Several lighter layers of clothing are better than one thick one, so that you can add or take off to regulate your temperature. Wool is much warmer than synthetic fibres.

The terrain of the Way makes its own local climate and, as the environment changes, it will be necessary to alter your clothing accordingly. If you wear shorts, carry warm trousers or breeches (not jeans) in reserve, to cover up against cold, rain, wind and sunburn, as well as nettles and midges. A windproof and waterproof anorak can be combined with a lightweight cagoule and over-trousers to protect you against the worst weather. Carry a woollen cap or balaclava, and take gloves, unless you are in a heatwave – when you will still need headgear for protection against the sun. Remember the spare sweater. Good hill-walking boots with moulded rubber soles are the most suitable form of footwear, along with several pairs of woollen socks – and spare dry pairs. Plastic and leather soles slip on grass slopes and wet rock and are dangerous. Anklets or gaiters are useful for keeping out mud, water and snow. Do not forget a spare pair of laces.

The route map, compass, whistle and a small first-aid kit are essentials and walkers should know how to use them. A simple blister left untreated can cause misery. Midge repellent can help to stop you being tortured between June and October, and a torch and spare batteries should be carried. A bivouac bag or large plastic sack could save your life in an emergency. Campers will have the heaviest burden as – apart from the tent – they will need a good quality sleeping bag, plus stove, fuel and cooking equipment.

A comfortable, well-packed rucksack is essential for all walkers – but try to avoid too heavy a load. Finally, if you plan to walk between December and April, an ice-axe could be a valuable friend.

Services and Supplies

Adequate supplies of food are essential to maintain energy. Your stores can be topped-up along the Way where shops are available, but they can be few and far between and hold limited stocks. Planning your supplies in advance is important. Day walkers can exist on energy foods such as jam sandwiches, chocolate and glucose, with a flask of soup, coffee or tea as a non-essential extra. The long-distance walker will need a greater variety of lightweight packaged foods. Water should not be drunk from burns or lochs below dwellings or in the neighbourhood of sheep and cattle pens, but in other circumstances the water is generally pure and safe. The services we take for granted in the city: banks, post offices, doctors and police – are less numerous along the Way and walkers should allow for this in their route planning.

Safety on the Hills

Follow the Mountain Code:

Think carefully before you go alone

Leave written word of your route with someone responsible and report your progress at the first opportunity

Plan within your capabilities

Know the local weather forecast

Watch the weather and adjust your plans wisely

Be properly equipped

Know how to use map and compass

Know the mountain distress signal – six regular whistles/flashes a minute, repeated at one-minute intervals

Know simple first-aid and the symptoms of exposure

Eat a little from time to time to maintain energy

Keep alert all day

In the event of accidents or emergencies, find the nearest telephone and dial 999, asking for POLICE.

The Country Code

Many people will walk the Southern Upland Way. The quality of their experience – and the welcome they receive – will depend upon the behaviour of those who go before them. Each has a responsibility to observe the Country Code, which is the key to ensuring happy relationships between walkers and those who live and work along the route.

Guard Against all Risk of Fire

The Southern Upland Way passes through substantial areas of woodland. Fires can start in forests and woodlands, and on grasslands and heather, at any season of the year – even in

25

winter. Fire is an indiscriminate and unpredictable hazard, endangering people, wildlife and scenery. It can destroy in a few hours, at great cost, that which has taken decades to grow. Camp fires should not be lit at all along the Way. The greatest care should be taken with stoves, keeping them well away from combustible material – and never, ever, left unattended.

Fasten all Gates
Where gates are used, fasten them securely behind you to prevent animals straying.

Keep your Dogs under Close Control
You are urged to leave dogs at home and not take them on the Southern Upland Way at all. The Way passes through lambing and stock-grazing areas at almost every stage of the journey and even docile dogs on a lead can upset stock very easily and cause great harm. Walkers will have enough problems on the Way without having to worry about the dog.

Keep to Public Paths across Farmland
The route of the Way has been agreed. There is no need to drift from the path into crops and pastures. Remember, grass is also a valuable crop to the farmer.

Use Gates and Stiles to cross Fences, Hedges and Walls
If walkers use the stiles provided it will not be necessary to clamber over fences and dykes, except where special crossing points have been built into the structure.

Leave Livestock, Crops and Machinery Alone
Machinery in the countryside can be dangerous. Try not to interfere with farming or forestry operations.

Take your Litter Home
Those on a single day's walk should take all their litter home. Walkers on longer outings should carry the minimum of tins and bottles, and dispose of them at service centres. Do not leave any litter in the countryside and try to avoid contributing to overflowing litter bins in rural areas.

Help to Keep all Water Clean
Numerous burns along the corridor of the Way supply individual houses or feed reservoirs for public water supply to communities within – and beyond – the Southern Uplands. Take care, particularly when camping, not to cause pollution.

Do not allow your rubbish or unused food to find its way into burns, lochs or reservoirs.

Protect Wildlife, Plants and Trees
Bring back photographs, not specimens. Avoid disturbing birds and animals and do not trample plants or young trees.

Take Special Care on Country Roads
The Way uses a great number of country roads. Normally they are very quiet but for your own safety keep well to the right side of the road facing any potential traffic, and be especially careful at corners. Wear light-coloured clothing or carry a torch in poor light.

Make No Unnecessary Noise
Going quietly will allow you to see more wildlife – and will add to the enjoyment of others. Loud transistor radios will not endear the owner to fellow-walkers or local inhabitants!

Enjoy the Countryside and Respect its Life and Work
Much of the enjoyment of the Southern Upland Way will come from meeting those whose livelihood depends upon the land you walk on. There is much to learn – and much to see. The psychological separation between town and country is slowly shrinking: the Southern Upland Way walker who is considerate will make a valuable contribution to an increased understanding between urban and rural dwellers.

Lambing
Walkers are asked to take particular care during the lambing season which stretches from January on low ground farms, to May on the hill farms. If ewes or lambs are encountered during this period, avoid at all cost disturbing them. Pregnant ewes can easily lose their unborn lambs if surprised or distressed. Please *don't* pick up 'lost' lambs: they're not. Go round rather than through flocks of sheep at all times. Stand still if sheep show signs of nervousness. Do not under any circumstances take dogs anywhere near them.

Cattle are also likely to be encountered on the Way and the same care should be taken with them. They tend to be curious and may advance rather than retreat! Don't panic and run – unless an animal is obviously aggressive. Cows and bullocks will frequently run up, stop and take a good look at you. Avoid excitement or you will transfer that to the animal also. In the event of meeting a bull, ram or other animal you are not sure of, go round it if possible with an eye to escape routes, or retreat and seek another path.

Grouse Shooting

Where the Southern Upland Way crosses grouse moors, please keep to the footpath – and during the grouse shooting season, which starts on 12 August, avoid disturbance to a shoot and risk to yourself.

Countryside Ranger Services

Borders Regional Council and Dumfries and Galloway Regional Council operate countryside ranger services based on the Southern Upland Way. If you encounter any difficulties or have comments or suggestions, contact:

Countryside Ranger Service,
Borders Regional Council,
Department of Physical Planning,
Regional Headquarters,
Newtown St. Boswells,
Roxburghshire.

Countryside Ranger Service,
Dumfries and Galloway Regional Council,
Department of Physical Planning,
Council Buildings,
Dumfries.

Ettrick

BEATTOCK—ST MARY'S LOCH

DISTANCE: 33km (21 miles)   HEIGHT RANGE: 90–525m

This is a long but fast section of the Way. Well-graded roads of various types are followed for much of the route, allowing a steady progress to be maintained. The Ettrick Valley is fairly remote and has few of the services required by the hungry, exhausted or benighted. Two days should be allowed for this stretch if conditions are bad. One or two farms may provide bed-and-breakfast but walkers need to plan ahead. Those wishing to break the section down into more manageable parts can travel by car to Dumcrieff Bridge or the Ettrick Valley. Camping is permitted at Cossarshill Farm, on the route 1km west of the Scabcleuch signpost. Seek permission at the farm, where a caravan is also available for let. Essential food supplies can be purchased at the farm. There are also two campsites further down the valley (east of the Scabcleuch signpost) – 4km (2½ miles) to Sagecroft and 7km (4 miles) to Honey Cottage campsites respectively.

Beattock and Moffat offer a range of accommodation and have bus links with the outside world and with each other, and Moffat has a taxi service. Beattock has a camp site. During the school term a bus service operates from Moffat up the Moffat valley to Birkhill. There is also a limited bus service called 'The Harrier' which operates on Tuesdays and Thursdays in midsummer along the Yarrow and Moffat valleys and over the Paddock Slack to Traquair. The bothy at Over Phawhope is available for use. Camping is allowed at Tibbie Shiel's Inn, by St Mary's Loch. Enquire there and not at the nearby sailing club where a number of caravans are parked.

Beattock is a small village just to the west of the busy Glasgow to Carlisle A74. South-bound vehicles go left and then under

The valley of the Moffat Water from the track up the Cornal Burn

this busy by-pass to reach the north end of the village, while north-bound vehicles cut off the A74 to enter the village at the south end.

Moffat is about 3km (2 miles) to the north of Beattock and is the main tourist centre for this locality, with a wide range of services, some fine buildings, and numerous features of interest. It is at the centre of an important sheep-breeding area and its Ram Fountain occupies a prominent position in the High Street. The town developed greatly as a holiday resort in the 18th and 19th centuries with the spreading fame of its mineral springs, which come from a sulphur-bearing shale. Hartfell Spa and Moffat Well are some distance from the town but in 1827 a suite of baths was built behind the new Assembly Room and water was piped to it from Moffat Well. One writer described the mineral water as resembling 'bilge water or the scourings of a foul gun' but people flocked to drink it for its reputation for curing rheumatism, gout, skin diseases and stomach disorders.

Robert Burns tried the waters and wrote several poems here. In Moffat House, designed by John Adam, James Macpherson resided in the 18th century while duping society with his Ossianic epic, supposedly translated from the Gaelic. James Boswell, dramatist John Home, David Hume, the renowned philosopher, and John Graham of Claverhouse all visited the town. The famous road-builder John Loudon McAdam is buried in the cemetery and Air Chief Marshal Dowding, who was born in Moffat and masterminded the Battle of Britain in 1940, is commemorated in a memorial in the Station Park.

With the opening of the Glasgow to Carlisle road through Beattock, Moffat became by-passed and a need arose for an inn farther west. Thomas Telford was responsible for designing the Beattock Inn, built in 1821. It had stables for 50 horses. As the Old Brig Inn, it is still in business today although the stable yard is now a car park. Above the entrance to the yard the archway still carries the message 'licensed to let Post Horses'. This fine Georgian building has an interesting stable block and sits at the north end of Beattock on the north bank of the Evan Water.

The Southern Upland Way drops down to Beattock from the west by the road from Kinnelhead entering by the south bank of the Evan Water. The bridge over the Evan Water carries a rounded sandstone tablet bearing the information: 'This bridge was built by John MacDonald from a plan by Thomas Telford in the year 1819'. A smaller tablet to the north states that it was 'widened 1951'. The Beattock House Hotel and camping sites are on the south side of the bridge, on the road into the centre of the village. The Old Brig Inn sits north of the bridge.

From the Telford Bridge over the Evan Water the Way passes the Old Brig Inn, then leaves the road by a lane to the east, north of the river. This leads by a cattle underpass beneath the wide concrete bridge carrying the A74 over the river, and up onto a minor road going east from the trunk road. The eastward walk is resumed along this road, crossing the Roman Road which went up Annandale and passing the site of one of their camps in a field to the south. Lochhouse Tower is seen to the north – a 16th-century stronghold of the Johnstones. It is a renovated and occupied three-storey tower. A more modern monument is an old Nissen hut by Barnhill House, just before the bridge over the River Annan is crossed.

The road splits left and right beyond the bridge – the left branch leading to Moffat – but the Way goes straight on over the ridge to rejoin the right-hand branch of the road on the other side. This ridge gives a good view for its modest height to Moffat and the sandstone spire and tower of two of its churches. Gallow Hill above Moffat had its height measured as 832 feet by Prof. George Sinclair in the 17th century, using a barometer – one of the first applications of this mapping technique in Great Britain.

To the left of the hill the Annan Valley recedes into the range, to the Devil's Beef Tub, where a very scenic road looks down into a former hiding place for stolen cattle, and passes a monument to McGeorge and Goodfellow who died in a blizzard up here in 1831 while carrying the mail. Both are buried in the cemetery in Moffat. As the Way passes over the ridge, we see John Loudon McAdam's mansion of Dumcrieff at the foot of the hill beside the Moffat Water.

Note – This route over the Oakrigg is closed annually from 15 March-15 May during the lambing season, when walkers should follow the road round the south end of the ridge. This adds an extra kilometre of walking but saves a bit of climbing. It also passes near the interesting feature of Threewater Foot, where the Evan Water, River Annan and Moffat Water team up to flow to the Solway as the Annan.

On the far side of the ridge the high route and road route meet beside the Moffat Water and follow it back to a junction and Dumcrieff Bridge. Just before the bridge there is another fine view over the wall of Dumcrieff House, McAdam's home around 1785. When he left the district it was first sold to Dr Currie, the biographer of Robert Burns, and next to Dr John Rogerson, who was appointed first medical adviser to the Empress and court of Russia.

Cross Dumcrieff Bridge and go left by a path into the beech wood. Beech trees carry a dense canopy of leaves in summer allowing little sunlight to reach the ground. In spring, before the canopy is formed, early flowers like wood anemone may be found at the foot of the beeches but thereafter little grows. Accordingly, in summer, the floor of Dumcrieff Wood is a thin carpet of short grass, brown leaves and beech-nut cases. The smooth grey girths of the mature trees are pleasant and impressive companions on this short stretch of the walk. The road runs parallel to the path only a short distance away on the right but the fresh, cool atmosphere of this woodland is not to be missed.

To the left is a conifer plantation of larch, spruce and pine and, towards the north end of the wood, other species of deciduous trees are associated with the beech, including sycamore, oak, holly and rowan, and rhododendrons take advantage of the uneven cover to spread themselves. When nearly out of the wood and opposite a white cottage, turn left and cross a small burn. This takes you into grazed parkland on the east bank of the Moffat Water. The river bank is followed upstream through agreeable surroundings of alder, sycamore, ash, lime, elm, willow and horse chestnut, until the minor road is met again where it crosses the river to climb up to join the A708 Moffat to Selkirk road.

The Way only crosses the minor road and continues upstream along the south bank of the Moffat Water through a field on a rough road. Then it crosses a second stile and turns at right angles away from the water, following the road along the north-east side of a belt of trees. The scanty remains of Cornal Tower are in the plantation opposite. This tower is associated with the unhappy Marion Carruthers who killed herself in preference to marrying a suitor chosen by her guardian.

Stay with the road as it crosses a cattle grid and takes a wide U-turn through a field, climbing above the Moffat Water valley and turning north-eastwards to follow up the Cornal Burn's valley on the south side. The view opens out to the west to Beattock and the busy A74, with Queensberry and the Lowthers behind. Moffat appears to the right over the ridge, as it is really in the valley of the River Annan rather than that of the Moffat Water. Swatte Fell looms to the north, with the very distinctive twin tops of Saddle Yoke to the right sweeping down into the glacial trench of the Moffat Water. Farther up, the valley is closing in to the unseen drama of the Grey Mare's Tail – one of the most spectacular waterfalls in Britain. Craigieburn in the foreground was the home of Jean Lorimer who inspired some of Robert Burns' poetry.

Continue upwards and eastwards on the road, entering the forest and following the south side of the valley of the Cornal Burn. When the valley turns to the south, follow the forest road across the burn to the north bank and continue along it north of the occupied dwelling of Craigbeck Hope. The road rises to the north-east again to pass over the col between Gateshaw Rig and Coomb Cairn and out of the influence of the Cornal Burn, then descends into the valley of a tributary of the Wamphray Water. Ahead of the road, three shoulders of Loch Fell running to the right lord it over the much smoother Birch Hill in the gap, which is forested in sitka spruce and lodgepole pine and has a prominent firebreak in line with the road.

The Way goes behind Birch Hill after curling down and round it on the south side, taking you into the steeply incised glen of the Wamphray Water. The forest road makes a U-turn across the Wamphray near the head of the glen and here the Way leaves the road and goes left up the first of three source burns. This is the longest and main source of the Wamphray but the other two start considerably higher on the slopes of Loch Fell. The stream followed by the Way rises on the col north-west of Loch Fell and its north-west top.

The scenery is very impressive cutting north to this col, with steep ridges hemming you into the floor of a narrow V-shaped valley. The plantations blend skilfully into the scene, feathering up the sides of the gullies and curling in natural style around the contours.

The Way is now approaching, by an old droving route, the col between Croft Head and Loch Fell, and the outside world seems a long way away, having been shaken off in a bewildering series of ups and downs, twists and turns and

The Selcoth Burn and the Craigmichen Scar of Capel Fell. The Way goes to Ettrick above the crags on the right changing of valleys. Even following a good forest road with few junctions, this area can be confusing for first-time visitors. Reference to map and compass at frequent intervals is advised, to remain in charge of your destiny. Avoid following the Wamphray to the south and remember that the goal of the route is to break through the hills to the north to the headwaters of the Ettrick. Although the route may appear unnecessarily long and twisting, there is no sensible alternative and it is really only the intimate and enclosed character of the glens which causes 'where am I?' doubts to arise at times.

The much sought-after col between Croft Head and Loch Fell is reached beyond the forest at a junction of valleys. Coming north-east to it across a level valley floor it is like stepping out onto a balcony and looking down to the Selcoth Burn. The col is a wind gap from which no burn issues to the north, and, astonishingly, even the massive northern slopes of Croft Head and north-west slopes of Loch Fell can produce no permanent streams in this direction either. Is the drainage pattern due to the dip of the strata? Has the Wamphray Water captured a head of the Selcoth Burn? Is the Wamphray Water eating down the ridge between Croft Head and Loch Fell and leaving itself liable in time to be captured by the Selcoth Burn? Or were other vital factors involved which have been cleared away by the glaciers so that we shall never know? There are problems here in plenty for geologists and students of topography.

Looking at the dangerously steep face of Craigmichen Scar on the side of Capel Fell across the valley, there is little sign of permanence. Thin beds of sedimentary rock protrude from the slope. Folding, faulting and erosion have riven the hill into high-angled screes and tottering outcrops. Vegetation clings precariously to the slopes, which display rank after rank of shallow terraces caused by soil creep. Diurnal variations of temperature between the warmth of the day and the cold of the night cause the soil to expand and contract and thaw and freeze. Gravity does the rest, pulling down the disturbed particles, slowly but relentlessly, centimetre by centimetre over a period of time. What looks like a sheep track across a slope is often a temporary terrace (though sometimes consolidated by sheep) caused by soil creep, in a brief respite in the destruction of the far from permanent hills.

The Selcoth Burn offers an escape route north-west to the Moffat Water and civilisation again, before the Way moves on. From a sheep stell (a 'ree' in the west) on the col, the route passes up to Ettrick Head along the right-hand slope above the deep gorge of the Selcoth Burn. Climb about 50m up the slope first to steer clear of the steepest drop, where a slip could be fatal. A small cairn is visible from the stell and is a good line to take you above the danger. The slope is still steep and requires great care and sensible footwear but should only present a problem to competent walkers in hard winter conditions. In such circumstances, if a safe way cannot be found higher up then it is better to retreat.

Once past the crags, the route descends to the burnside and turns the corner of the valley to look ahead towards Ettrick Pen. The views can be spectacular to the west and south on this section but assume a more rounded, duller character as the Way crosses the Selcoth Burn at a bridge and heads straight over the slope north-eastwards to the left of the peaty col of Ettrick Head. With snow on the hills and good visibility, it is no exaggeration to say that the views around the Selcoth Burn can compare favourably with many of those in the Scottish Highlands. There is a Glen Nevis-like character about the gorge and the surrounding hills, making this stage one of the great highlights of the Way. It would be a pity to miss the best of the experience by seeing it on a poor day.

One cannot live for ever on highlights, so we are back to more mundane slopes at Ettrick Head where the regional boundary fence cuts across the path at the col. As the Selcoth Burn winds back to lose itself in the peat hags, the watershed of Southern Scotland is crossed and the Borders Region entered – a highlight after all!

The Selcoth flows to the Moffat Water, which in turn joins the Annan to flow to the Solway Firth and the Irish Sea. At the north end of the peat hags is the source of the Ettrick Water, which flows north-east to the Tweed and the North Sea. The Tweed is one of Scotland's greatest rivers. It dominates the Borders and here is the proof, as its tentacles meet us on our first few steps into the region. The journey outwards is well over for the Southern Upland Way walker going east from Portpatrick. You are coming in now!

The Way crosses the col on the north side of the peat hags and leads to a stile over the regional boundary fence. The fence runs across the col from Capel Fell to Wind Fell and can be seen as a double fence running up the ridge of Loch Fell, separated by a broad corridor of ground. Is this a 'no man's land' relic of the past? Did drovers establish this route from time immemorial as a right of way, to avoid the steep slopes along the Selcoth Burn? Whatever the answer, the Way follows the valley floor north-east into the forest from Ettrick Head on the left side of the infant river. A forest road is soon joined and the uphill route to the right taken. The left route

Ettrick Pen from Over Phawhope

appears to be heading directly for the valley but isn't! The right-hand route swings round the side of the valley and soon shows itself as the better line. The boundary dyke along the ridge from Capel Fell to Graham's Law is conspicuous above, as is a cairn on Hopetoun Craig ahead of the forest road. A nearer cairn on Midden Hill, west of the Ettrick, marks a bend in the valley and road and river round it on a northerly course. The white walls of Potburn Farm can now be seen. The road loses height more gradually than the Ettrick, which is cutting ever deeper into the landscape, capturing tributaries from every slope, and growing quickly into a sizeable stream.

The problems of tree-planting are interesting here. The narrower ridges look down on radial strips of planting, while broader slopes have allowed rectangular blocks to be created. We are back to sheep country again as the stone cottage of Over Phawhope is approached. The cottage has been renovated by the Mountain Bothies Association with the consent of the owner and is left unlocked to provide overnight shelter for the weary walker. It has a living room and a dormitory. Anyone using it should keep it tidy and respect

The Ettrick Valley at Potburn

the goodwill of the owner and the volunteer renovators who made its use possible.

The road fords the river here but a wooden bridge takes walkers over. It is inscribed 'Constructed by ITP 66 SQN RE'. The road leads on past Potburn where a side track goes over the hills to Bodesbeck on the Moffat Water. The Way slants uphill to the north-east, past a large grey shed to join the public road to Ettrick at a large turning and parking place.

There are 8km (5 miles) of tarmac road to be walked down the valley now but it is an easy and pleasant walk, on a normally quiet single track, with passing places. Parking spots are scarce so it is mainly used by locals, rather than by tourists who have to drive on in frustration, unable to stop at the beauty spots they see. Parking is of course prohibited in the passing places. While it may appear harmless to leave a car on such a quiet road, it can cause chaos when, by an unfortunate chance, a large vehicle such as a cattle float meets two cars just at that point!

Between Potburn North and Broadgairhill there is a fine view up-river to Graham's Law, with a mature stand of scots pine on the south bank and larch on the north. Below Broadgairhill the valley becomes more populated and cattle join the sheep on the hillsides. Nether Phawhope has another group of tall scots pine standing above a little gorge on the Ettrick, to add great character to this river and contrast with the backcloth of plantations and open slopes.

Maps of this area have 'Ettrick Forest' printed in large type across them. The name is an ancient term and has nothing to

Graham's Law and the Ettrick Water from above Broadgairhill

do with modern commercial plantations. The area was a royal hunting forest for centuries, where Scottish monarchs relaxed in the brief intervals between battles, intrigues or affairs of state. The little pockets of pine surviving along the river bank are descendants of a great natural forest which sheltered William Wallace as an outlaw in the late 13th century. Edward I sought to add Scotland to his English kingdom at this time and would have succeeded had not a few patriots like Wallace held out to keep the country in unrest. Without the forest, Wallace would not have stayed free for long.

It is easy to look on valleys such as the Ettrick and conclude that grassy slopes and sheep farms were the natural order of things before the tree plantings came along. Change, though, is as endemic in the country valleys as in the towns, if not more so. Towns rarely disappear from sight. However, north-west of Over Kirkhope, by the Kirkhope Burn, there are traces of a now-vanished village and an ancient church. A carved stone from there, dating from the 5th or 6th century, is on permanent display in the Dark Age Sculpture Gallery of the National Museum of Antiquities.

The Ettrick Water at Nether Phawhope

Road and river run together past Crook Cottage. Only a low turf dyke separates the two to keep inattentive drivers from plunging into the water, and to prevent the rain-swollen river from overflowing across the road. The valley has widened at this point with the build-up of alluvial terraces but beyond Brockhoperig it is restricted again. The scree-strewn Craig Hill blocks the route ahead, with a cairn standing out above the littered slopes.

The Ettrick cascades over a sill under a line of alders and turns eastwards as a lusty young river past Ettrick Kirk 2km (1 mile) off the Way. The Way is now leading over the hills to Tibbie Shiel's Inn, so it is relevant to know that Tibbie the innkeeper is buried in Ettrick churchyard, along with other notables including James Hogg, who was born near the churchyard and has a monument by the road on the site of his birthplace.

Hogg lived from 1770–1835 and is widely remembered as 'The Ettrick Shepherd'. Herding sheep is a difficult trade to follow but not likely to lead to fame. Hogg was far from outstanding among herds, but he wrote poetry – and society

The Monument to James Hogg

pretends to understand that. Robert Burns had died in 1796 when Hogg was just starting on his literary path. Like Burns, Hogg came from a working background where lessons and reading had to be fitted in after the essentials. Perhaps the nation was seeking a successor to Burns, perhaps Hogg's verses were outstanding for their time, but more likely it was the friendship of Sir Walter Scott which set him on the way to fame and literary success. Scott was a far-travelled man in his duties as Sheriff of Selkirkshire and pursuing his own interests. He met often with this literate herd from a neighbouring parish and grew to enjoy his company. With Scott's friendship around him, Hogg found the way into print easier and he began to write prose as well as poetry. Although many Scots learn the name of James Hogg, few read his works today – a fate also befalling the great Sir Walter himself.

Hogg at his best was outstanding and among his greatest works is *The Private Memoirs and Confessions of a Justified Sinner* – an astonishing psychological thriller away ahead of its time. Although the Way does not go past Hogg's birthplace, it is entering Hogg territory and we shall hear more of him soon.

As the Ettrick Valley and road turn east to Ettrick village, the Way leaves both at Scabcleuch, where a Scottish Rights of Way Society sign points out the route to the left to St Mary's Loch, running steeply uphill on the west bank of the Scabcleuch Burn. A gate at the top of the field leads to a rough road going off to the left. Avoid this and continue ahead along a shelf west of the burn, losing height relative to the burn until you are almost at the point of the V-shaped valley, without being in the burn!

Little waterfalls grace the burn, while in late Spring, primroses cling to the steep banks avoided by sheep and cattle. Two sheep-folds and a small broken cliff are passed and the slope eases back to the col across rough and moist clumps of grass and reeds. Despite the upland appearance of the valley, pheasants erupt from under your feet. The cairn on Craig Hill is very prominent, looking back, while Ettrick Pen dominates the view to the south.

A fence crosses the col with a gate and stile on the west side and a stile on the east side. Another Scottish Rights of Way Society sign stands at the stile, pointing forward to Riskinhope and back to Ettrick Kirk across the higher slopes and another col. This route descends the Kirk Burn to Ettrick – evidence of the worshippers who crossed the ridge from Riskinhope in the past. The gate leads to yet another SRWS sign, giving a three-way split at a junction with the other path. This sign points back to Scabcleuch and Ettrick Kirk and ahead for both routes to Riskinhope through hill grazings dotted with Blackfaced sheep.

The Riskinhope route is taken along the east side of Peniestone Knowe. When the falling ridge on the left is almost level with the path on Pikestone Rig, the right fork in the path is taken near a sheep-fold and above a ruined barn in the valley. The left fork crosses the Rig on its way down to Riskinhope and the A708 at the Loch of the Lowes, while the Way, following the right fork, runs on along the east side of the Rig towards the Wiss – a big hill behind Riskinhope Hope. Not far from the Loch of the Lowes stands Chapelhope, the setting for the Ettrick Shepherd's *Brownie of Bodsbeck*. Renwick, the Covenanting preacher, held a meeting above Riskinhope in 1688 shortly before being caught and executed in the Grassmarket at Edinburgh.

The novelty of the names here reinforces the changes of identity met in crossing the uplands. Each region has its own landscape, character, culture, social history and problems – and the Southern Upland Way walker is in a unique position to appreciate them at every change of scene.

Having walked under Graham's Law and up the

Scabcleuch Burn, the walker will appreciate that a 'law' is another name for a hill-top in this region and that a 'cleuch' is a narrow, steep-sided valley. 'Rig' has been met before in Galloway and is short for ridge, but 'hope' is a distinctly east-side term meaning a valley with a meandering burn.

Riskinhope to the west is a farm at the foot of the Riskinhope Burn. Riskinhope Hope would normally be an enclosure or steading at the head of the Riskinhope valley but for some strange reason it stands on the Whithope Burn, which then changes its name to the Crosscleuch Burn. There are problems in plenty to be sorted out in southern Scotland by those interested in place names! Some discrepancies on the map may have originated from the problems of communication and interpreting dialect between the locals, and the map-makers from perhaps three or four hundred miles away. Some perhaps through the map-makers being unfortunate enough to ask the wrong local who, either in a moment of senility or sheer cussedness, gave the wrong information. The names given to all the local features were essentially oral ones and those who did the naming died long ago. Their creations have been translated onto paper and handed down from map to map through the centuries, complete with spelling mistakes and embellishments to frustrate and puzzle the knowledge-seeker thereafter.

The Way descends from the end of Pikestone Rig, steeply down to Riskinhope Hope which is a derelict sheep farm falling into ruin like its shelter-belt of conifers. Drystone-walled boundaries mark out the in-bys, tilting up the slopes in both directions from the valley, while nettles cluster about the door of the house. The slopes on the east side of the valley are forested now, with wide breaks left to allow sheep access to and from the hills. The Whithope Burn is crossed below the house and the path taken to the col between Earl's Hill and Fall Law. The view is fine from here to the south-west over the house. Ettrick Pen stands out beyond the valley which is patterned nearby with extensive drainage ditches.

At the col a stile is crossed into the forest, where several signs point the route to Riskinhope Hope and to Hopehouse on Ettrick Water by the Captain's Road. This is an old drove road which we follow in the opposite direction, crossing a ford by boardwalk and joining an old Selkirk County Council made-up road which heads north-westwards to St Mary's Loch.

Away over the valleys ahead stand some of the highest hills in the Southern Uplands. Broad Law, Cramalt Craig and Dollar Law stand in a line above the 800m mark, and are numbered second, third and fifth in order of height in Percy

Donald's Tables of Hills in the Scottish Lowlands, 2000 feet in height and above. Broad Law and Cramalt Craig also feature as two of the nine Southern Upland hills to earn a place in J. Rooke Corbett's list of Scottish Mountains 2500 feet and under 3000 feet in height. Dollar Law is omitted from Corbett's list as, under his criterion, it was only an outlying top of the higher Cramalt Craig. Five of the 'Corbetts' were passed in Galloway and two were seen north-east of Moffat. The Tables by Donald and Corbett are published by the Scottish Mountaineering Trust, along with the 3000 feet 'Munros'.

The hills seen to the west are sometimes known as the Tweedsmuir Hills. When the writer and statesman John Buchan was elevated to the peerage, he chose as his title Lord Tweedsmuir, from his fondness for these hills and the great river on the far side which the Way will come to later. To the left of Broad Law, the steep cleft down to Talla Reservoir is glimpsed briefly as the road drops and the distant views are replaced by St Mary's Loch as the descent is made from forests and sheep country to a much more varied pattern of land-use. Despite the height of the uplands, the mountains here and elsewhere have been ground down to a peneplane, deeply dissected by valleys such as at Talla and the trough of St Mary's Loch, now being approached.

Along the side of the road, outcrops of dark grey shale break down to thin angular screes littering the reddish-brown soil. At a bend in the road, a bridge bears warning notices to drivers that it is unsafe to take a car across. Details stand out clearer in the valleys now. Beyond the farm of Crosscleuch stands Tibbie Sheil's Inn on the flat area between the Loch of the Lowes and St Mary's Loch. Both lochs would be joined at one time but alluvium brought down by the Oxcleuch from the west, and the Crosscleuch and Thirlestane Burns from the east, have built up deltas separating the lochs now, save for the small connecting stream running under the bridge to Tibbie Shiel's from the main road. Beyond this road stands the monument to James Hogg at the left edge of a wood. His dog Hector sits at his feet, while the poet holds a scroll bearing one of his most famous lines: 'he taught the wandering winds to sing'.

Hogg was a frequent visitor to Tibbie Shiel's Inn, among a coterie of notables, including Sir Walter Scott and Christopher North. Christopher North was the pen name for John Wilson, a professor of moral philosophy at Edinburgh University and an editor of Blackwoods Magazine, to which he contributed some of his celebrated 'Noctes Ambrosianae'. This series of essays included material gleaned from his stays

44

at Tibbie Shiel's, where he came every autumn with his family.

Tibbie lived from 1782–1878. Her molecatcher husband appears to have lived a quiet, undistinguished life, but on his death, Tibbie built up a wide reputation as a good innkeeper, entertaining some of the most eminent figures of the day – whose praises led others to follow. Her husband, Robert Richardson, is buried with her in Ettrick churchyard.

The inn still functions today. The main road is a short walk west from it, over Tibbie's Brig and the smaller bridge on an overflow channel to its west. The Way turns right at the inn and enters the surroundings of the St Mary's Loch Sailing Club. The Loch of the Lowes to the south is a much smaller loch than St Mary's and is much less deep.

The glacier moving north-east down the valley from Moffatdale was a weaker force than that formed by the union of the Megget and Moffat ice-streams half way down St Mary's Loch. In the ice jam at that corner, the combined glaciers bit deeper into the base rock to form a trench, now filled with 46m of water. The Loch of the Lowes is 18m deep at its maximum. The deep U-shaped valley of the Little Yarrow runs back from the Loch of the Lowes to the col at Birkhill, where the road crosses the regional boundary and descends to the south-west past the Grey Mare's Tail. This is a 60m high waterfall dropping spectacularly from the moraine-dammed Loch Skeen high in its corrie in a hanging valley. The waterfall and loch are in the care of the National Trust for Scotland.

Birkhill Cottage displays a plaque on the outside wall, commemorating Charles Lapworth, a Galashiels school-teacher whose geological discoveries in the Moffat area helped to untangle the complexities of the study of the earth's crust. Lapworth began to study fossil graptolites in the rocks. These extinct marine invertebrates, by their development over periods from the Cambrian to the Carboniferous, have allowed geologists ever since to identify certain rock beds wherever they came upon them. It was Lapworth's work in Dobb's Linn on the Moffat Water, and at the impressive Craigmichen Scar, passed a short distance back along the way, that unlocked the Silurian and Ordovician (his term) periods that are so important in the structure of the Southern Uplands.

Birkhill was once an inn and a Covenanters' haunt like the Watch Knowe above the road. Claverhouse is said to have executed four Covenanters near the inn at another time that is momentous in the story of the Southern Uplands.

Dryhope Tower and St. Mary's Loch

Yarrow

ST MARY'S LOCH—TRAQUAIR

DISTANCE: 19km (12 miles) HEIGHT RANGE: 160–475m

The walker now has a fairly short and straightforward section, given reasonable weather, with a road never very far away. However, public transport is very sparse. There is a daily bus service in each direction, Monday to Friday, between Innerleithen, Traquair, the Gordon Arms and Selkirk, while a school bus during the term does a double run from Innerleithen and Traquair to Glenlude. The Harrier Scenic Bus Service and Border Courier Service connect St Mary's Loch with the Gordon Arms, Traquair, Peebles and Selkirk every Tuesday and Thursday from July to the start of September.

At St Mary's Loch accommodation is available at Tibbie Shiel's Inn and the Rodono Hotel. Tibbie Shiel's Inn has a field for campers. At the other end of this stretch, walkers may have to look beyond Traquair to nearby Innerleithen to find accommodation. There is a camp site at Innerleithen, as well as hotel and bed-and-breakfast. Most of this stretch is along a footpath, which occasionally becomes indistinct.

Tibbie Shiel's Inn is a busy corner on a summer day as tourists, anglers and sailing enthusiasts go about their pleasures. A commemorative plaque here marks the site of the official opening of the Southern Upland Way in April 1984. It is only a short walk from the A708 to Tibbie's at the south end of St Mary's Loch and many take that stroll, whether they intend to visit the inn, fish or sail. The Way goes past the front door of the inn to the gate into the St Mary's Loch Sailing Club. This is a right-of-way and walkers should not be confused by the sign stating 'Members Only'. The track is followed over a stile and past the clubhouse to the loch-side.

The east bank of the loch is followed northwards past a splendid green area of tall fir, larch and pine at the mouth of the March Sike. Oystercatchers, common sandpipers and mallard frequent the loch-side and great crested grebes can be seen gliding along the water. The Rodono Country Hotel sits opposite Bowerhope Law, with its conical turret in the corner of its red-brown and grey sandstone and whin walls.

The combination of an elongated loch filling the valley, the high ridges above, modulations in tree-cover, variegated slopes of grass and heather, colourful sailing craft, and ever-changing nuances of sky and sky-reflections, make this a most attractive walk through a celebrated area of great landscape value. Scott writes a very fitting description of it in *Marmion*:

> 'Oft in my mind such thoughts awake,
> By lone Saint Mary's silent lake;
> Thou know'st it well, – nor fen, nor sedge,
> Pollute the pure lake's crystal edge;
> Abrupt and sheer, the mountains sink
> At once upon the level brink;
> And just a trace of silver sand
> Marks where the water meets the land.'

Traffic flows along the far side of the loch but the walker can enjoy the south bank in peace among its wildlife and sheep. On the maps of Roy and Edgar (1747–55) and (1741) the road runs along the north shore of the Loch of the Lowes and then crosses to follow the south shore of St Mary's Loch.

The loch bends opposite Cappercleuch where the Megget Water has pushed out a large deltic fan of alluvium into the loch. This has now become stabilised and colonised by plants and grasses to make a flat green sward. Just opposite the delta, St Mary's deepens steeply where the Megget and Moffat glaciers united to tear into the valley floor.

A road runs through the Megget Valley to the high district boundary at the Megget Stone before descending spectacularly to the Talla Reservoir, which was constructed between 1895–1905 to supply water to Edinburgh. The Megget has its own dam now. In 1977, work started on creating a new reservoir for Lothian Regional Council. The dam, at 56m high, is the tallest in Scotland. It is a gravel-fill embankment dam 568m long, grass-sown on the downstream side, which can be seen from the Way across St Mary's Loch. The first stage in the project involved the construction of the dam and a tunnelled aqueduct north to the head of the Manor Valley. From there a pipeline carries the water via the Meldon Hills into the supply area, through Gladhouse Reservoir, Glencorse Reservoir and Roseberry Filters.

In the second stage of the project, a pumping station will be built on St Mary's Loch at the edge of the Megget delta and

48

water will be pumped from the loch into the reservoir. Sluices at the outlet of St Mary's Loch will control its level. Recreational facilities will be provided along the north side of the reservoir for angling, sailing, picnickers and walkers, with car parks, laybys, toilets, viewpoints, and information signboards.

In *The Bridal of Polmood* James Hogg describes a royal hunt meeting on Hunter Hill above Cramalt Tower, with upwards of 400 men driving the deer from Blackdody to Glengaber and the Dollar Law into the royal trap above the castle, with archers, seventy leash of hounds and one hundred greyhounds assembled for the slaughter. Hunter Hill can be seen from the Way as it passes up St Mary's Loch, opposite the early 19th-century church at Cappercleuch and the Megget Valley. The direction changes here under Bowerhope Law, turning more to the north-east.

Opposite Bowerhope and under Capper Law is the graveyard and site of the now vanished St Mary's Chapel, which also features in Hogg's writings. The chapel was of great age. William Wallace is said to have been appointed Warden of Scotland in it in 1297. An annual service called 'The Blanket Preaching' is held here in July and is thought to have originated in conventicles of the 17th century when Covenanting ministers had a blanket held over their head in inclement weather – the chapel being ruinous by then. A traditional tale tells of a chaplain of St Mary's being shot for dealing with the devil, while the ancient ballad *The Douglas Tragedy* ends with its eloping lovers being buried here. A tall ash and three smaller trees up the hillside distinguish this historic and romantic spot for us across the loch – but anyone seeking to unravel fact from fiction faces a frustrating task.

Bowerhope is skirted along the loch-side to join the road out to the end of the loch. The London-born novelist and poet, Maurice Hewlett, wrote his book *The Forest Lovers* while staying at Bowerhope. He resigned his post as Keeper of Land Revenue Records in 1900 to devote himself to writing, and he published historical romances, essays and poetry, including *The Song of the Plow*. The road out from Bowerhope runs under plantings of larch, with a lighter growth of birch and other species along the loch-side, leaving the view open to the north and Dryhope Tower which is seen across the haugh at the end of the loch.

The haugh has been built up by deltas forming out from the Kirkstead and Dryhope Burns. With the Thorny Cleuch Burn from the south, they have dammed the loch's outlet with alluvium raising the water-level, although this is now controlled by man. In the 19th century Lord Napier had sluices built at this end of the loch to conserve the water supply for the mills at Selkirk, which had previously lost production in summer droughts. Now this end of the loch will be reconstructed again under the second stage of the Megget scheme.

The main influence on the scenery was, of course, the ice-sheets which swept over the col from Moffatdale and down Megget to gouge out a rock basin and form this long loch in the first place. As the Yarrow Water leaves the loch, it winds its way round and through heaps of morainic litter on its journey north-east to join the Ettrick.

While the country south and east of Ettrickbridgend and Selkirk is pockmarked with kettle-hole lochs, St Mary's is the last sizeable natural loch that the Way-walker will meet on the route east to the sea. The granite of the west is solid and indented enough to hold numerous sheets of water – but the softer rocks of the hills to the east erode more quickly and let the water escape. With a drier climate, there is also less water falling to collect and to attempt to hold in the east. The greater peneplanation beyond Ettrickbridgend and Selkirk gives that area a more confused drainage pattern, with more standing water.

An unusual event took place at Dryhope in the 1780s, when Vincenzo Lunardi came floating over the hills in his gaudily coloured balloon and attempted to land at the Haugh. Lunardi was an Italian aeronaut who had created a sensation by making the first hydrogen balloon ascent in England in 1784. Cashing in on his novelty-value, Lunardi toured the country demonstrating his balloon before multitudes of sightseers. Our erratic climate brought him to Dryhope from Glasgow, where he attempted to anchor and land but the wind carried him off again, to set him down eventually by the Ale Water.

The Way rounds the east end of St Mary's Loch at a bridge over the Yarrow, then follows the north bank of the river downstream for a short stretch to a footbridge over the Dryhope Burn and so by a stile on to the main road. To the left, the road heads for Moffat and Megget. To the right, the road goes to Yarrow past the Gordon Arms where James Hogg and Scott met for the last time in 1830. Scott was two years from death and Hogg five, as the old friends took their last walk together. Above the hotel sits Mountbenger where Hogg farmed unsuccessfully. To the south is Eldinhope (then called Altrieve) where he died. As the Way reaches the road, walkers have Altrieve Rig behind them.

Cross the road, go over a stile and follow the dyke up the left edge of two fields between two green sheds until the track from Dryhope to Blackhouse is joined.

Wherever one goes in this countryside there are historical, literary and romantic associations, and Dryhope is no exception. The yellowing 16th-century peel tower of Dryhope stands above the colder grey workaday stone of the neighbouring farm. In afternoon or evening, when the light is behind the tower, throwing shadows into prominence, the patterns of outbuildings or enclosures show up in the grass below the tower, while there are traces of hut circles just to the west.

The tower was the birthplace in 1550 of Mary Scott – 'The Flower of Yarrow' – and wife of 'Auld Wat of Harden' from whom Sir Walter Scott claimed descent. 'The Flower' is associated with providing her husband with the legendary meal of a pair of spurs, served up on an otherwise empty ashet. This was a powerful hint that, if he wanted his supper, it was time he got on his horse and raided some more cattle – as the larder was bare. Auld Wat was implicated in the Raid of Falkland in 1592, when the Earl of Bothwell besieged King James VI in his palace. Dryhope and Harden were destroyed as punishment but both were rebuilt again.

The Way joins the cobbled track north-east of the tower and turns uphill between two fences towards a conspicuous cairn on the skyline. The main track follows the Dryhope Burn but the ancient long-distance route taken by the Way cuts off from this to the north-east and passes under the cairn through the gap known locally as the Hawkshaw Doors.

Ancient earthworks crown the Mid Hill which sits in this gap and looks back in a splendid view to Dryhope, St Mary's Loch and the Ettrick hills. The Way goes through the gap to the north-west of Mid Hill, passing left of a sheep-fold, then dropping slightly to cross a tributary of the Douglas Burn by a plank bridge. Go round the foot of the South Hawkshaw Rig, staying on the left edge of the valley. The route can be seen in the distance climbing past a plantation at Blackhouse.

Pass left of a sheep-fold and turn up the valley coming down between the Hawkshaw Rigs until a bridge is found across the Hawkshaw Cleuch. A gate and stile above the far bank are good markers for the bridge, which is partly hidden by birch and hazel. North Hawkshaw Rig is now contoured about 30m above the valley floor and the bluff opposite Blackhouse is followed until a path leads down to a bridge over the Douglas Burn.

There is not much left of Blackhouse Tower today as it sits among trees surrounded by farm buildings. It is said to have been a Douglas stronghold for centuries and an older tower on the same site was thought to have been used by the Good Sir

James Douglas, who played a valiant role along with Bruce in the struggle for Scottish independence in the early 14th century. Sir James was also called 'The Black Douglas' supposedly because of his swarthy complexion, and it is possible that Blackhouse derives its name from this. The map today shows the Douglas Burn flowing past the door, from its source in the Blackhouse Heights bordering the Manor Water to the west.

A traditional ballad *The Douglas Tragedy* tells of Lady Margaret Douglas fleeing with her lover Lord William, pursued by her father and her seven brothers. A fight reputedly took place on the Bught Rig in which all nine men died or were mortally wounded. The six-inch Ordnance Survey map shows a ring of seven standing stones and another ring of six Douglas Stones on the Bught Rig, but the remains of these features are rather indeterminate now. Lady Margaret died, presumably of grief, shortly after Lord William, and both, according to the ballad, were buried in the old kirkyard above St Mary's Loch.

James Hogg was shepherd at Blackhouse for ten years and met the greatest blizzard in his experience while working there. In *Storms*, Hogg gives a vivid account of the menfolk from Blackhouse searching for sheep in a blizzard which filled the cleuch between the Hawkshaw Rigs so deeply that the tree-tops were covered.

Willie Laidlaw, the son of Hogg's employer at Blackhouse, was ten years younger than Hogg. Together they helped each other to learn and to cultivate an interest in poetry and the traditional tales of the Borders. Laidlaw passed on some of this knowledge to Sir Walter Scott when Scott came visiting, and began a lifetime of service and advice to the great man, becoming his amanuensis or copy secretary and steward. It was through Laidlaw that Hogg later became friendly with Scott.

Take a look up the Douglas Burn towards the Douglas Stones and the head of the glen which was once worked for gold, then cross the bridge and follow the track between Blackhouse Farm and barn and up the left-hand side of the old plantation. This is an old road from St Mary's Loch to Traquair, Peebles and Edinburgh, shown on Will Edgar's map of 1741, and called the 'Muir Road' on Roy's map a few years later. Beyond the plantation of varied mature trees, the route goes through new plantations above the Craighope Burn. The track is well graded and leaves the forest at a stile and gate at the district boundary on the ridge.

St Mary's Loch is still seen behind, but new territory opens up ahead, with the Paddock Slack road between Traquair and the Gordon Arms, the Moorfoots beyond the Tweed Valley, and the bare Minch Moor standing above the forests ahead where the walk will soon go.

Looking more immediately north, a sheep-fold can be seen across a small valley which runs down to Glenlude. This sheep-fold is a guide for the next kilometre, moving north-east down an ill-defined ridge, with hollows, grassy foundations, raised boundaries, and demarcation of the grasses showing where an old settlement once stood to the right. A tributary of the Glenlude, known as the Yellow Mire Burn is crossed south-east of Deuchar Law and a track taken uphill to pass left of the sheep-fold and the cairn disclosed to the north of it. Another cairn becomes visible to the left on the north slope of this ridge. Head left, passing above the cairn and dropping north-west to the right edge of the saddle where a gate and stile will be found.

Those going south from the saddle will see two cairns up on the left. Go above them and turn right over the top. The stile into the forest should now be visible across the shallow valley, which is crossed to gain the ill-defined ridge. Once at the stile, the Way looks to the Mid Hill and St Mary's Loch, which is the line to take to stay on the drove road.

A well-constructed coach track continues north-east from the saddle, slanting up through the heather to Blake Muir. It becomes banked on both sides and makes a distinct notch on the skyline below the summit. Dun Rig stands high to the west in front of the other Manor Hills, while Mountbenger to the south-east beyond the road shows a prominent cairn on the summit and one on the north slope. A fence comes in on the left of the drove road and both pass through the gap just left of the summit of the hill.

A wide panorama is seen to the north, with the spa and woollen town of Innerleithen prominent at the juncture of two valleys with the main Tweed Valley. Lee Pen is a pointed peak, just off the map, to the left of the town. Arable fields and woodlands lead up to green pastures and forests, while the heather-patched Moorfoots range along the background.

The first mill in Innerleithen was established in 1790 but the town rose to prominence, like Moffat, through the discovery of its mineral springs. It was Scott who made its reputation when he published his novel *St Ronan's Well*. Whether he had Innerleithen in mind as a setting or not is debatable but Innerleithen seized its chance and took the name 'St Ronan's Well' for its spa. It even persuaded royalty to drink the sulphur water giving it the right to erect a royal crest over the spa pavilion. Visitors to the town today enter past a sign stating 'Innerleithen and St Ronan's Wells'.

The River Tweed runs past the town, so even if the river is difficult to see from Blake Muir, at least the valley is now visible and another point of the walk is reached. With hills in all directions it is easier to see from here how the old county of Peeblesshire, now being crossed, had a higher mean altitude than any of the counties in the Scottish Highlands. As a completely land-locked county it did not drop to sea-level at any point.

The track is taken down the north-east ridge of Blake Muir with the Glen to the north-west. The Quair Water issues from its wooded valley, which starts as a dry valley glacial meltwater cut, from the end of which the spring-fed Loch Eddy passes into the river. The Scottish Baronial-style mansion of Glen House was designed by David Bryce and is well seen from the ridge. During the last war valuable paintings from the National Gallery of Scotland were stored here in the cellars, as a precaution against bombers. This is grouse shooting country and red and black grouse can be seen on the Way. Walkers should be prepared to be asked to wait on Blake Muir or Fethan Hill while a grouse drive takes place after August 12th. The heather is left behind at a gate and the track continues through pastures along the crest of the ridge. Fethan Hill features in Hogg's tale *The Witches of Traquair*.

The track moves over to the right, close to a small spruce plantation at the end of this field, with a dozen roughly circular barrows or ancient grave mounds just west of the track. The next field is descended diagonally to meet the dyke coming in on the right after executing an L-shape. Cross the dyke and go along the edge of the fields, keeping the dyke on your left. The path passes through gorse and nettles to a vehicle track, descending to join the B709 at some houses just south-west of Kirkhouse.

The road is now followed north-eastwards to Traquair, past the parish church which was erected in 1778 and altered in 1821. It is an attractive building, oblong in plan, harled and slated, and has an outside stair and an open bellcote and two original round-headed windows. The burial aisle of the Stuarts, Earls of Traquair, is attached to the north wall. Seventeenth-century tombstones in the yard show that an older church stood here before the present building. Some of the grave memorials are carved with skulls, crossbones and an hour-glass. One to a gardener at Traquair shows his spade and rake while a 1902 memorial to a Major-General in the Bengal Cavalry shows some of his military kit. George Scott Moncrieff is buried here, remembered as 'author, poet, playwright, patriot 1910–74'. Alexander Brodie's mortal remains lie in Middlesex but his nephews and nieces

Traquair Church

subscribed for a memorial to this Traquair-born ironmaster, which credits him as 'the first inventor of the Register Stoves and Fire Hearths for Ships. Had the honour of supplying the whole British Navy with the latter for upwards of thirty years to the preservation of many lives since their introduction and was a great saving to Government. Died 6 January 1811 aged 78 years'.

The barns at Kirkhouse and Orchard Mains make an interesting contrast, while a lodge opposite the road to the latter has an 1867 datestone over the door and a Victorian post-box. As the road nears Traquair village, it takes a sharp bend to the right. An old lade is seen to the left of the bend, running back to the river from the 18th-century Traquair Mill. Then the first houses are passed and the Way turns right up to the Minchmuir, opposite a large and impressive pink sandstone war memorial cross. The entrance to Traquair House is down the road to the left past the war memorial and over the Quair Water and the 1770 Knowe Bridge. It is a major attraction of the region and should be seen by those who have the time, energy and opportunity.

Traquair House claims to be the oldest inhabited house in Scotland. Twenty-six Scottish and English kings have sheltered here since the visit of Alexander 1st in 1107. At that time the castle would be a timber construction and, through the following turbulent centuries, it developed and was rebuilt into a stone peel tower on to which bits were added at the sides. The last major alteration took place in the 17th century when the building was unified under a new roof, giving it its unique appearance – a distinctly Scottish chateau.

The 'Steekit Yetts' or closed gates at the end of a long avenue of sycamores are involved in legend. One story has it that the 5th Earl closed the gates behind Prince Charles in 1745, with the promise that they would never be opened again until the Stuarts were restored to the throne. Another version is that they were closed on the death of the 7th Countess, while it is even said that the gates cannot open, being made as only a decorative unit.

The house contains an outstanding collection of treasures, including 16th-century embroidery, silver, porcelain, old manuscripts and relics of Mary Queen of Scots. The 18th-century library is almost intact, while the Priest's Room has a secret stairway for escape. The 18th-century brewhouse has been restored and Traquair Ale is now produced under licence and is available to visitors.

The cottage tearoom also provides light meals and snacks to visitors while home baking is on sale from the bakehouse. The gardens include nature trails, woodland walks and a maze. The house and grounds are open from Easter to October in afternoons, and mornings and afternoons in July, August and early September.

Traquair House was a strategic base for royalty, hunting in the Ettrick Forest, and many impressive processions must have wended their ways over the route followed by the Southern Upland Way. The Marquis of Montrose came hammering on the door in 1645, unsuccessfully seeking admission. His royalist army had just been defeated at Philiphaugh by General Leslie, and Montrose had only escaped by hurrying over the high Minchmuir road – and that is the route which the Way will now be taking. For the tired walker, Innerleithen – with its accommodation facilities – is only 2km (1 mile) or so away.

The Minchmuir

TRAQUAIR—YAIR BRIDGE

DISTANCE: 15½km (9½ miles)   HEIGHT RANGE: 120–525m

The Minchmuir is a very enjoyable walk – not too long, not too high, and not too difficult. The middle section is exposed so it should not be tackled in bad weather by inexperienced walkers, nor indeed in very bad weather by even experienced walkers. An acquaintance of James Hogg died in the snow here, so it demands some respect. In good weather the only problem should be staying on the route through the forest sections and that need not be difficult. The conditions are fairly firm throughout, so a good speed is possible and strong walkers may wish to push straight on to Galashiels or Melrose. Cars can be parked at the village hall in Traquair, and, less easily, on the verge near Yair Bridge if the conditions are not too soft. Motor-cyclists and horse-riders are sometimes encountered on the walk but, mostly, walkers will have it to themselves. While there may be little accommodation available around Yair Bridge at the end of the section, Clovenfords and Selkirk are not too far off and the A7 bus route on the north bank of the Tweed is only 3km (2 miles) away – bringing Melrose, Galashiels or Selkirk well within bedding distance. At Broadmeadows, 1½km (1 mile) off the route, there is a youth hostel. Alternatively, walkers could continue along the Way, beyond Yair Bridge, to Galashiels (5km–3 miles) where a range of accommodation is available.

From the cross-roads at Traquair village, go south-east opposite the war memorial and follow the minor 'no through road', past the village hall. Leave the road where it bends right to the school and continue straight on up the hill on a rough cobbled vehicle track. A hedge on the right offers brambles, wild raspberries and gooseberries in season, while an ash on the left has a twisted limb spiralling tightly around its trunk.

The track becomes grassy but widens as it passes through fields, curling up left into the forest. The view over Traquair House to Innerleithen is good, with the triangular Lee Pen standing boldly above the town and its mills. The River Tweed is seen twisting through its tree-clad valley before the dense forests near at hand shut off the view and upward progress is made between close-pressing larch and spruce.

The forests are modern additions but the track is ancient. The Minchmuir route is an old road which was in use as far back as the 13th century. Edward I is said to have crossed it with his army when conquering Scotland. It is marked on Roy's map (1747–55) as the 'Peebles to Selkirk' road. Sir Walter Scott's mother crossed it in a coach and six when a girl, to attend a ball at Peebles, although footmen walked alongside to make sure the coach stayed on the road. Sir Walter brings the Minchmuir into his writings in *The Two Drovers*.

In olden days, robbers were said to frequent the Minchmuir in wait for unsuspecting travellers. Modern travellers prone to nervousness need not dwell on these things for too long among the dense conifers, however. A field on the right, at the planting stage, gives a clear view again. The V-valley of the Quair Glen stands out, backed by green, yellow and brown field patterns and the heather-clad Manor Hills.

Cross a forest road and continue straight up the track between tall conifers again. This leads to another forest road running along the contours. Cross it and carry on uphill. The pine and spruce at this stage are heavily undergrown with heather, which eventually takes over as the track leads out to open hillside – a very colourful area in late summer. The track leads round the left side of the top of the hill to the Cheese Well. This is a spring about 10m right of the track and is marked by two stones. One is roughly rectangular and the other diamond-shaped. Both are inscribed 'Cheese Well' and one bears the date 1965 and an emblem with a thistle head in the centre.

According to tradition, travellers passing the Cheese Well made an offering of cheese or other food to the fairies or spirits of the well. This altruism stemmed from a desire for security, as anyone facing the elements, the discomforts and the bandits of the Minchmuir didn't go looking for trouble from the 'wee folk' as well. Anyone wishing to uphold the tradition should do so with restraint and not allow the well to become a midden of rotting food!

The track passes north of the summit of the Minch Moor

The Cheese Well

(567m) which lies about 1km (½ mile) south but only about 54m higher than the track. The ascent can be made easily to the cairn by a path marked by ageing wooden posts. A firebreak left of the Way looks down through the trees to Walkerburn in the Tweed Valley with the undulating Moorfoot Hills beyond. A mill at Walkerburn houses an interesting museum of wool textiles. Looking north-west over the trees, the red-roofed Hydro can be seen on the edge of Peebles. The Hydro was originally planned for Innerleithen, to exploit the mineral wells there, but the laird would not agree to it, so it went to Peebles – which does alright for itself as a major tourist centre. It has numerous shops, ancient monuments like the Cross Kirk and Neidpath Castle, historical and literary connections with Mungo Park and John Buchan, Chambers the publishers, and numerous services and scenic walks for the visitor.

The track descends slightly now as it heads south-east, crossing the district boundary into Ettrick and Lauderdale with trees on both sides of the route. A slight bend to the left reveals the north and central peaks of the Eildons with Berwickshire beyond – the final district for the east-bound walker! The little pinnacle left of the Eildons on the mid-horizon is Smailholm Tower, standing on its volcanic crags, where Sir Walter Scott stayed as a boy, learning the stirring Border tales from his grandfather which he was to weave into his writings in later life.

The Way descends a wide heather band between the plantations, to a col where a forest road cuts across it on a skew from the south to the north side of the ridge. Cross the road and follow the heather band up and across the south side of Hare Law. On the green floor of the valley below sits the house of Lewenshope Hope amidst a group of pines, while south-east and south-westwards lie the Cheviot and Ettrick hills.

The track branches at the next col to the east. The Minchmuir road takes the right-hand and downward trail to the Yarrow Valley where Broadmeadows and Newark Tower show above the trees. The Way takes the left fork and stays up on the ridge, heading for Brown Knowe. Yarrow is at the centre of the Border mystique, through traditional ballads and songs and the writings of Scott, Hogg and others. Wordsworth made the valley the subject for three of his poems.

The Scottish Youth Hostels Association's first hostel was opened at Broadmeadows in 1931. Prior to the event the opening party walked over the Minchmuir. In 1981 the Golden Jubilee of the Association was commemorated with a repeat of the walk. Now the SYHA has 80 hostels, open to anyone over the age of five.

Newark dates from the 15th century and was used by Scottish kings as another base for hunts in the Ettrick Forest. It features in Scott's *Lay of the Last Minstrel* and is best known as the setting for a grisly deed, the repercussions of which we have seen all along the Way in the pathetic martyrs' tombs. In the Civil War, the Royalists led by the Marquis of Montrose, and the Covenanting Army led by David Leslie, met in battle in 1645 at Philiphaugh just downstream from Newark. The Royalists were surprised and routed. The victorious Covenanting Army showed no mercy to their prisoners. Remembering the slaughter of defenceless citizens in Aberdeen by Montrose's wild supporters, they herded their captives into the courtyard at Newark and butchered them. Meanwhile, Montrose fled over the Minchmuir road and was rattling on the door of Traquair House seeking admission. The laird pretended to be not at home and Montrose moved on to escape to Norway.

In 1649 Charles I was executed and Montrose came back to Scotland a year later in support of Charles II. The venture was hopeless, his army was again routed, and he was taken to

Edinburgh and executed. So James Graham, 1st Marquis of Montrose, who had signed the Covenant in 1638, was hanged by the Covenanters 12 years later. Such are the complexities of Scotland's bloody history.

The splendid woodlands in this part of the Yarrow hide Bowhill, one of the homes of the Duke of Buccleuch and Queensberry. The 1st Duke of Buccleuch was also the Duke of Monmouth and natural son of Charless II and was beheaded in 1685 for his part in the unsuccessful rebellion against James II of England. Bowhill is open to the public and displays Monmouth relics as well as many magnificent treasures of furniture, porcelain and silver, and paintings by Canaletto, Gainsborough, Reynolds, Raeburn and many others.

The Direction Stone to Wallace's Trench

The A708 passes the site of the 1771 birthplace of Mungo Park opposite Newark Castle. Park qualified as a physician and practised in Peebles but the love of travel was strong in him. In 1795, 45 years before David Livingstone set foot in Africa, Park was exploring the course of the River Niger. That, as Way-walkers will now appreciate, was less than 50 years after General Roy set out to systematically map the tiny country of Scotland. Park suffered great dangers and difficulties in Africa and was imprisoned for four months by a hostile chief before escaping. On his second expedition to the Niger he explored 1000 miles of the river and was tragically drowned in it while being attacked by tribesmen.

As the Southern Upland Way climbs the crest of Brown Knowe from the west it crosses near the summit what is known as 'Wallace's Trench'. This is a linear earthwork running north to south over the ridge, and heading steeply down to cross the Minchmuir road as well as it loses height on its way to Yarrowford. The earthwork comprises a ditch and an upcast bank on the west side. The upper track also crosses a smaller north-to-south ditch slightly to the east. A small stone at the Minchmuir road is inscribed 'Wallace's Trench 300YRDS'. That the two tracks run through gaps in the upcast ridges suggests that the earthworks were constructed to control traffic on the roads and not to block them completely. They may have served some administrative rather than warlike purpose – and probably had nothing to do with Wallace, whom they may well pre-date. When it is remembered that Wallace lived in the 13th century and map-making did not develop much before the 18th century, it will be understood how mysterious derangements in the landscape, for want of a rational explanation, came to be associated by a simple populace with a legendary hero. Like the De'il's Dyke, passed in Galloway, Wallace's Trench is just another of the many riddles standing under the sun, moon and stars to baffle us along the Way.

Three fences meet at the summit of Brown Knowe just to the east of Wallace's Trench. The Way stays high, following the ridge line to the east, towards the striking Three Brethren cairns above the forest. The fence goes north of east, while the path stays a bit south of the fence to avoid a rough and boggy area. There are spacious views to the Yarrow over three ridges as the path turns down the slope through heather to the col east of Brown Knowe. This spot is known as Four Lords Land. The view is restricted to the north but the valley to the south is interesting, with a number of broken dykes running steeply up the slopes, dividing the ground into rectangular field patterns. There is an easy escape route from the Way

The Eildons from the Three Brethren

here by a path down to Yarrowford and Broadmeadows, the latter with its youth hostel.

The col is crossed at a gate above a ragged, wind-damaged fringe of trees and the vegetation underfoot changes dramatically to bracken and, in summer, lush green grass. Nettles and irregularities in the ground at the corner of the field suggest that this site may have once held a dwelling. Follow the north-east side of the dyke upwards now, staying west of the crest of the ridge but still above the fringe of mixed tree species. Another gate leads to a contour across the slopes north of Broomy Law, still on the north side of the wall.

Clovenfords is conspicuous to the north-east, over the Yair Hill Forest, with a very straight section of the A72 heading towards it. John Leyden, the Scottish poet and orientalist, was schoolmaster here in 1792 before travelling to the east and acquiring 34 languages. In a short but very full life, he found time to translate the gospels into five languages. Scott and the Wordsworths also stayed here and a statue of Scott stands in front of the Clovenfords Hotel. In 1868, the Duke of Buccleuch's head gardener started a vinery here which developed into an industry yielding 15,000lbs of grapes a year. Clovenfords had its own railway station up to 1962 on the Peebles to Galashiels line.

Ashiestiel Hill to the north of Broomy Law stands above the Tweed Valley, as does the unseen Ashiestiel House where Sir Walter Scott lived from 1804–12. As Sheriff-Depute of Selkirkshire, he was legally bound to reside in his Sheriffdom for at least four months every year, so he took a lease on this house and used it for eight years before moving to Abbotsford.

Also out of sight in the valley behind Elibank Law is Elibank Tower – the setting for one of the best legends of the Borders. It concerns Willie Scott of Harden, the son of Auld Wat and the 'Flower of Yarrow' whose exploits we were reminded of at Dryhope near St Mary's Loch. According to the story, Sir Gideon Murray of Elibank had caught Willie stealing his cattle. Willie was offered a choice – a hanging or a marriage to Sir Gideon's ugly daughter 'Muckle Moothed Meg'. Willie took one look at the ugly Meg and chose the hanging, but relented in time to save his neck. Records confirm that the two did marry, but whether under the circumstances described who can tell, over three centuries later? The legend has inspired Hogg and Browning, as well as a play by Alexander Reid.

No matter where you look, every corner here seems to have its story in this area so incredibly rich in traditions, legends, history and culture. Even the ancestors of Franklin Delano Roosevelt, the 32nd President of the USA, came from Philiphaugh. Mungo Park must have climbed Foulshiels Hill many times. It is inconceivable that the great explorer of West Central Africa would not know this 443m summit just 1km (½ mile) from his home. Lower down on Foulshiels Hill is the grave of Tibbie Thomson, who was driven to hang herself by the cruel tongues of her neighbours.

Some may walk over Broomy Law and think that the Southern Upland Way is a dull walk, with no splintered peaks or vertical precipices to astound the observer. To the initiated, it is an enthralling saga that is gradually disclosed over its length. It is the very story of Scotland that is laid open – free from the decoys of tartan imagery and the maudlin sentiments of performing hucksters. Ironically, we are now entering the Scott country, and it was Sir Walter more than anyone, who popularised Rob Roy and things Highland, which led to the unjust neglect by many people of other parts of Scotland.

From the wall north of Broomy Law, the Way continues along the ridge. A path goes off south to Broadmeadows from the col and is another escape route, but the Way carries on east, up the edge of the forest to the Three Brethren. There are three cairns, 3m high – one in each of three properties which meet here in a terminus of fences. The lands of Selkirk Burgh, Yair and Philiphaugh come together here at the summit.

The inhabitants of Selkirk jealously guard their rights in the Common Riding. This is a ceremony held annually in June, when riders go round the Marches or bounds of the Royal Burgh in a colourful procession. Each trade or corporation has its own flag and standard-bearer in a ceremony at least 400 years old. Selkirk has statues of Mungo Park, who served his apprenticeship as a doctor in the town, Scott, who was Sheriff here for 33 years, and Fletcher – the only one to return – according to tradition – from the Battle of Flodden in 1513, out of eighty who set out. Four and a half centuries have not eradicated the terrible impact of Flodden on the town, and the Common Riding is a commemoration of those who died. The riders' route goes out by Linglie Hill to Tibbie Thomson's grave, then up to the Three Brethren and back to Selkirk.

The view from the Three Brethren is dominated by the triple peaks of the Eildons standing above the Tweed Valley. The Tweedbank industrial estate is easily seen between Galashiels and Melrose while Black Hill at Earlston is prominent. The Moorfoots still line the northern horizon but now the big regular line of the Lammermuirs is seen clearly to the east. As the last major upland feature to be crossed on the Way, the walker has further confirmation of progress.

The Way descends south-eastwards between the fence and the forest to the col at Peat Law. Yet another track goes to Broadmeadows from here. Turn left in the other direction and follow the track down through the forest to join a wider forest road. Cross this road to join 'Red Score Nick', a path through the trees which dips and then climbs, before turning left downhill to join another stretch of forest road. Go left on this about 100m, crossing a small burn, then turn off to the right by a footpath through the trees again.

This leads to the edge of the forest. Going west on this section, fork left at a junction of rides. The route down follows just inside the edge of the forest between a meadow on the left and the deep valley of the burn on the right. Riders obviously use this path and cannot enjoy the trailing hawthorns overhead, but the banks are rich in flowers and grasses in summer.

The Way joins the estate road at the kennels and stables at Yair, in a sharp right turn past a Scottish Rights of Way Society sign. The present house at Yair was built in 1788

Yair Bridge and the River Tweed

while the lodge farther east dates from 1820. The walker has now reached the far-famed River Tweed and follows it a short distance downstream from the lodge. An old mill lade can be seen on the far bank, which disappears through Yair Bridge to the mill-site. The walker arrives at the bridge from the other bank and crosses over on to the junction of the A707 and B7060 at Fairnilee.

Yair Bridge is a three-span rubble construction with segmental arches, cutwaters and refuges for pedestrians. Its age is not known but the act authorising the building of the road was passed in 1764. Its builders could never have foreseen the advances in transportation which were coming. Today, it carries an 11-ton weight limit and is too narrow to take two vehicles passing. An interesting feature is the mortise and tenon jointing of the stonework, seen on the parapet, while there is an Ordnance Survey benchmark in one of the refuges. There are good views in both directions along the Tweed from the bridge.

Gala

YAIR BRIDGE—MELROSE

DISTANCE: 12km (7½ miles) HEIGHT RANGE: 85–275m

A short and partly urban section of the walk within the capabilities of novice walkers and family groups, and need only exercise the experienced for a few hours, leaving them time to see some of the interesting places in the area. The walk passes through a great variety of scenery, from the ugly to the beautiful, and follows paths, tracks and roads by riverside, hilltop and old railway line.

There is a great variety of accommodation available in the Galashiels and Melrose area, including a youth hostel at Melrose. Both towns are served by local and long-distance bus services.

This part of the walk starts at Yair Bridge, where the A707 Selkirk to Caddonfoot road crosses the River Tweed at the junction with the B7060 to Galashiels. Just west of the bridge, a Scottish Rights of Way Society sign points out the public footpath to Galashiels which the Way follows. This goes left of Fairnilee farmyard, following a track uphill into a wood. Fairnilee House is seen on the left in the gap of the Tweed Valley. It is a 1908 mansion (architect: J. J. Burnet) which has superseded an ancient seat of the Ker family. It was here that poetess Alison Rutherford wrote her lyrical version of *The Flowers of the Forest* in the 18th century. She married Patrick Cockburn, an advocate, and became a queen of Edinburgh society.

After crossing the tarmac estate road, the Way continues uphill on a fenced track between arable fields. The view opens behind to the Tweed Valley and the Three Brethren above the forests. The three Eildons are bold to the south-east and much nearer now. The track forks at a plantation. Go right and then cross pasture land, still following the track to the west of the house at Calfshaw. A small burn is crossed in a dip and then a steep track fit only for a tractor leads to a gap between two plantations of pine and larch on Hogg Hill. Hard ribs sticking out of the sides of Neidpath Hill to the left show that the grass is only skin deep in this green and beautiful landscape.

Piles of stones accumulated in the fields hint again at the untidy state the glaciers left the countryside in after the last Ice Age. Selkirk is visible now across the Ettrick Valley. A textile town and former shoe-making centre – whose inhabitants are still called 'souters' after the trade they used to follow – the former burgh has a long history. In 1113 Earl David (the future King David I) founded an abbey at Selkirk. There was a royal castle here, and, disputing the claim of the chapel above St Mary's Loch, it is said that William Wallace was proclaimed Overlord of Scotland in the old kirk in the 13th century. A curfew bell tolls nightly at 8pm from the steeple and there are museums of old ironmongery and relics of Sir Walter Scott and other local material at Halliwell's Close and the Courtroom. Selkirk's connections with Mungo Park, Scott and Flodden have already been mentioned and the town's pride in its traditions is very evident in its Common Riding. 'Better to be a lamp-post in Selkirk than the Provost of Hawick' is a local conceit, while another states that 'a day oot o' Selkirk is a day wastit'.

The Yarrow and Ettrick rivers team up above Selkirk, near Philiphaugh, and will shortly join the Tweed. A television mast stands high above the town – one of several seen from the Minchmuir. Ruberslaw is seen left of Selkirk. It was a Roman signal station and another Covenanters' retreat. The bigger hills , from Cauldcleuch Head to the Cheviot, stand out along the Border, emphasising that although the Southern Upland Way is travelling north-eastwards, England is getting nearer all the time.

Go north-east from the plantation gap, with the dyke on your right, towards the left of a scraggy-looking plantation. Bear to the left between knolls in the field before reaching a dyke with an old 'through-band' stile, and cross the dyke by the stile. The route at this point is traversing improved pasture between the rougher heather slopes above on the left and the lower arable fields on the right. Galashiels is seen left of the plantation from the crest of the hill – a town of grey-walled buildings, wrinkled mill-roofs, a green-roofed school and a red-spired church. The Black Hill of Earlston is prominent to the right.

The ridge has been crossed now, the Tweed left behind (for a time) and the descent is made to the Gala Valley, aiming for

Galashiels from the track across Gala Hill

the left end of the wooded Gala Hill which hides the east end of the town. Just beyond the larch plantation, the Eildons and the Tweed Valley are seen again on the right. Stay left of the dyke but well above a pond in the valley, crossing a transverse dyke by an inbuilt gap, left of a gate. Another gate leads through a wood to emerge at the bottom end by a stile. A linear earthwork runs through the wood and is popularly referred to as the 'Catrail' or 'Picts Work Dyke'. It was thought at one time that this represented part of a fifty-mile construction from the Gala Water to the Cheviots but this view is now rejected by archaeologists.

While there are many stretches of earthworks between here and the Border and we have already met one at Wallace's Trench – there is no hard evidence to link them into a lengthy tribal frontier. Present-day archaeological detectives are hampered by centuries of misuse of the evidence. Old roads and field boundaries, and the total destruction of the evidence by ploughing, either laid false clues or obliterated real ones. It has been established, though, that the earthwork crossing the Way ran southwards from Galashiels to Rink Hill above the

Galafoot Bridge over the River Tweed

Tweed and possibly farther. Like the De'il's Dyke and Wallace's Trench, it gives the Way-walker much to think about concerning the landscape as it is seen today, and the way it would have looked – and the reception the walker would have received – many centuries ago.

From the end of the wood the track descends to the north-east across a field. A minor road to Galashiels is low down on the right. A dyke comes in from the left at a group of old trees and this dyke is followed to the edge of the wooded Gala Hill. A high wall is turned on the south and east and a path leads through the trees north-east, to the minor road leading you into the outskirts of Galashiels. Those going in the opposite direction leave this road at a sign stating 'Public Footpath to Yair Bridge'. East-bound walkers follow the road round Gala Hill past the first houses of the town and take the first turning right (Barr Road) for the continuation of the walk.

Galashiels is the centre of Scotland's tweed manufacturing industry. The first carding machine in Scotland was erected here in 1790. The town developed along both banks of the Gala Water and, with water power and locally produced wool, the community thrived. The four-storey 19th-century Valley

Mill still has its beam engine house while the Scottish College of Textiles, founded in 1909, has an international reputation in the fields of textile technology and textile design. The town still has its mercat cross, restored in 1887. Old Gala House dates back to about the 16th century and has a 17th-century painted ceiling, though much of the house is later than this. It is now an arts centre.

The best-known feature of the town is probably the statue of the mounted Border Reiver, by local artist Thomas J. Clapperton. The term 'Reiver' is much associated with the Borders. A reiver was a 'moss trooper' or, less politely, a robber or freebooter. The statue stands in front of Sir Robert Lorimer's very impressive clock tower war memorial. The tower chimes out a curfew every evening at 8pm with the notes of *Braw Lads o' Gala Water* – a Robert Burns song which has been adopted by the town. The 'Braw Lads Gathering' takes place every summer and originated in 1930. It follows the older traditions of the Common Ridings in other Border towns and one of the highlights of the 'Gathering' is the ride-out to Sir Walter Scott's home at Abbotsford, fording the Tweed and returning round Gala Hill by the road which the Southern Upland Way takes into the town.

As the Way turns up Barr Road, it is contouring the northern slopes of Gala Hill above the town. The tarmac road leads across the hill and up out of town again, to a cobbled track going past an electricity sub-station. This tree-lined lane leads to benches and a wide view to the east. There is a stone tablet cemented into the end of a dyke at an iron gate. The inscription reads: 'Here Roger Quinn Author of the Borderland Gazed on Scotland's Eden from the Spur of Gala Hill.' What would Quinn have thought of the council housing estate, the gas works and the factory units of the new industrial estate today? Nevertheless, it is a splendid view along the Tweed to Melrose and the Eildons grow in stature every time they are seen.

Go through the gate and continue along the edge of the field with the dyke on your left heading south. Once over a slight rise, Abbotsford appears, surrounded by woodlands, with the Eildons behind. Turn left at the end of the field alongside electricity transmission wires coming over the hills from the right and almost immediately disappearing into the ground. Without them, the view improves to the Tweed and the new A7 from Carlisle, to which the Way is dropping.

Continue down the track with the dyke on your left towards the big house of Brunswickhill with its tower and flagpole. A lane to the left of this house brings you to Abbotsford Road which was once the main road between Galashiels and Selkirk

Abbotsford across the River Tweed

but is now quiet enough for car parking. Cross the road and
continue the descent at the concrete bollards closing off a
minor road. Cross the new A7 with care – as it is considerably
busier than the old one – and follow the minor road down to
the old railway and the minor road beyond it along the river.
We are back to the Tweed, following it downstream, walking
on the edge of the road or on the bank to the right wherever
possible. This is a beautiful stretch of the river enhanced by
splendid beech trees.

Abbotsford appears across the river and now we are truly in
the heart of the Scott country. Sir Walter bought part of this
estate in 1811 when it was a farm called 'Cartleyhole'. He re-
named it Abbotsford from the crossing on the river and set
about reshaping it to his liking. He was still working on it
when he died in 1832. The original house was demolished on
his instructions and the present structure built to the designs
of Edward Blore and, later, William Atkinson about 1816–
24. No doubt Sir Walter would make a fastidious client,
adding suggestions here and refinements there, so that the
end result today is not the coherent idea of one brain.

Nevertheless the building is a major piece of Scottish architecture and initiated the Scots Baronial style which flourished in Victorian times.

Sir Walter's patronage of Blore saw the architect off to an illustrious career, with commissions for restoring Glasgow Cathedral and several English cathedrals, and appointment as architect to the Crown with work engagements at Hampton Court and at Buckingham and Windsor Palaces.

Sir Walter all the while was decorating his estate and house with beautiful woodlands and gardens, and books, armour, weapons and relics, from models of Bruce's skull to bits of stonework and panelling 'rescued' or copied from historic buildings. At Dalry, as readers of Volume I of this Guide will recall, Sir Joseph Train was stopped just in time from 'acquiring' the St John's Chair for Sir Walter. In 1826, disaster struck Scott. The publishing house of Ballantyne went bankrupt, with debts of around £100,000. Scott, as a business associate of the firm, resolved – to his eternal glory – that no one should suffer financial loss through him. He redoubled his energies in writing, producing book after book and wearing himself out in the process. The debts were paid off – but Sir Walter was physically wrecked and he died at Abbotsford in 1832 at the age of 61.

Today, Abbotsford is open to the public from late March to the end of October. Visitors can see the grounds and gardens, the private chapel added after Scott's death, the entrance hall, armouries, dining room, library, drawing room and study where Scott worked himself to death. It was in his study at Abbotsford that he wrote most of his Waverley novels, *Old Mortality*, *The Heart of Midlothian*, and so on.

At the time of his purchase of Cartleyhole, the Tweed's banks were almost treeless and it is Scott we have to thank for starting the planting programme which makes the area so attractive today. His influence was immense on Scotland, not only in literature, law and politics, but in social habits and on the environment, as millions have visited the places associated with his writings, while other landowners have copied the landscaping improvements he made to his estate.

As the Way moves down the opposite bank of the Tweed, we look across to the back of Abbotsford. The Tweed is a river which can claim to have inspired more writing and poetry than any other in the country. Inland from the Tweed and the Way, the bed of the branch railway line from Selkirk to Galashiels accompanies us on the left. An old red-painted iron footbridge crosses a cutting to Abbotsview Convalescent Home, near the site of Abbotsford Ferry Station. The railway line was opened in 1856 and closed to passengers in 1951.

The Abbots Ford at Kingsknowe has been replaced by a high, slim concrete and steel road bridge carrying the road between Galashiels and Melrose. This 'Galafoot Bridge' was opened in 1975. It has an overall length of 193m and is 22m above the river, with two main spans of 60m and two smaller side spans. The superstructure comprises four welded steel plate girders carrying a reinforced concrete deck slab. The reinforced concrete piers consist of a single shaft with a hammerhead cross-beam. The bridge cost £1½ million and was designed by Sir Alexander Gibb & Partners.

As its name suggests, the Gala Water joins the Tweed just beyond the bridge. Before the junction the two rivers are running parallel to each other in opposite directions. The scenery becomes distinctly urban beyond the bridge, where the river bank has been cleared for a car park and picnic site. A feeder road comes down from above and the Way goes on by the riverside road, into an industrial corner of Galashiels containing a council yard, the former gas works and sewage works. Left of the road is an area called the 'Englishmen's Sike' where, in 1337, a party of marauding Englishmen were surprised and cut down by locals. At that time, Edward III was winning back much of Scotland from Robert the Bruce's weak successor, David II. The Englishmen, according to tradition, had stopped to pick wild plums – a bitter delicacy in view of the outcome. The town of Galashiels has as its motto: 'Soor Plooms.'

Beyond the gas works, the Way crosses the road bridge over the Gala Water and passes the sewage works situated between the two rivers. The road runs on into a housing estate but the Way turns down a surfaced path to the right, to join the former 'Waverley' line opened by the North British Railway Company from Edinburgh to Hawick in 1849, and advanced to Carlisle in 1862. In 1876, the Midland Railway reached Carlisle via Settle and the Waverley route was complete and in competition with other routes to England. Branches were thrown out from Fountainhall to Lauder, from Peebles to Galashiels, and Galashiels to Selkirk, while from St Boswells other lines traversed the Merse of Berwickshire, linking up with the East Coast main-line. The Waverley line was a stiff test for locomotives, with severe gradients and the Gala Water crossed sixteen times. Through the 20th century the branch lines were gradually cut back until, in 1969, the Waverley route itself was closed, despite strong opposition and the take-over of a level crossing, by villagers at Newcastleton to stop a London train. Today, the Borders are completely devoid of railways save for the East Coast main-line from Edinburgh to London on which no trains stop within the region. The loss of the trains has had an incalculable effect on the Borders, including a dramatic increase in car ownership through necessity, while winter travel has become much more hazardous.

After the brief but unattractive walk through service areas walkers are glad to get back to the country again. From the rail viaduct over the Tweed there are good views along the river, then the railway trackbed is followed eastward past a plantation and the Tweedbank housing estate. Leave the tarmac as it goes to the houses and continue with the rail-route as it curves through a cutting framing the Eildons.

Wooden steps are taken to the left on to Lowood Road and the road followed right, past plantations and fields left of Tweedbank industrial estate. This minor road emerges at the A6091 where it runs on to Melrose Bridge. Mind the traffic and cross the road to a stile into a field, heading to another stile and footpath along the south bank of the Tweed. The Waverley Castle Hotel shows an impressive roof-line on the right above some magnificent trees. It is built on Skirmish Hill, where it is claimed the last clan battle in the Borders took place in 1526. The hotel was built between 1869–71 and is said to be one of the first concrete buildings in Scotland. The site was chosen wisely, then being convenient for the railway, Abbotsford and Melrose, and as it developed as a hydropathic establishment, it was in great demand by the Victorians. It has a white statue of Scott in its grounds.

The river is easily followed now to Melrose, though it generally requires pretty fast walking to travel at the same speed as the current! The path is good through riverside meadows, emerging at a kissing gate on a bend in a road. Leave the road immediately to the left and the path climbs above the river with a wall on your right, to arrive on Weir Hill at a grassed area in front of the 1810 parish church. This makes a convenient entry point to the centre of Melrose.

A monastery associated with St Cuthbert was established at Old Melrose around the year 650. Melrose Abbey was founded in 1136 by David I. It was the first Cistercian abbey to be built in Scotland and became the parent house for many others, spreading its influence westwards into Galloway to Glenluce and up into the Highlands. Considerable wealth accrued to the monastery from the practice of breeding large flocks of sheep, and from this time onwards the Scottish landscape underwent fundamental changes in its vegetational cover as scrub forests were cleared and the rudiments of farming established. The abbey was changing greatly itself, suffering along with the monks in the turbulent Wars of Independence and being continually rebuilt. Situated on one

Melrose Abbey

of the shortest routes from England to Edinburgh, it was particularly vulnerable. The red sandstone ruins seen today show some of the finest flamboyant stonework left in Scotland. The rich window tracery, flying buttresses, pinnacles and carved figures make this ruin worthy of close and detailed study. The church is vaulted throughout and has north-facing cloisters – both unusual features in Scotland. The Commendator's House is the only relatively intact part of the abbey now and is used as a museum. An ingenious drainage system makes use of the waters of the Tweed as did the abbey mill. There are many interesting graves here, including the heart of Robert the Bruce, returned after Douglas's death in seeking to take it to the Holy Land. Also here are Alexander II, the Douglases, and Michael Scott the Wizard. Michael Scott was a 13th-century philosopher, traveller and student of the natural sciences. He dabbled in alchemy and other practices which might have earned him a fiery end from the authorities in another age. He was knighted by Alexander III and was attached to the court of the Emperor Frederick II. He translated Aristotle and features in Dante's *Inferno* and Sir Walter Scott's *Lay of the Last Minstrel*.

Eildon North from the Monument at the Roman Fort site of Trimontium

Melrose has many other claims to fame. It was here that the seven-a-side rugby game was born, and the town has a 17th-century mercat cross. Priorwood Garden is a National Trust for Scotland property specialising in growing flowers suitable for drying. It has an attractive orchard with an 'Apples through the Ages' walk. The garden is adjacent to the abbey and has a visitor centre, shop, and information service. The youth hostel is in the same area, while near the Abbey Mill is a motor museum. 2km (1 mile) east of Melrose at Newstead is a monument erected by the Edinburgh Border Counties Association on the site of the important Roman camp of Trimontium, built by Agricola in AD79. After excavations in 1905, the site was filled in to preserve it. The Eildon Walk is a not too strenuous diversion, taking in Melrose Abbey, Newstead and the North Eildon where there was an Iron Age hill-fort.

The Eildons were formed by volcanic activity millions of years ago and not, as legend would have it, by Michael Scott the Wizard commanding the Devil to split them into three. Terraces are visible on the north slopes, some showing signs of cultivation rigs, and it is thought that a considerable population inhabited the north-east hill-top town or fort before the Romans arrived. Traces of 296 circular houses have been identified here. The Romans took over the site for a signal station and lookout post but built their camp at the foot, at the spot called Trimontium after the three peaks. Sir Walter Scott is reported to have said that he could stand on Eildon Hill and point out over forty places famous in war and verse.

At Dryburgh, farther down the Tweed, is another of the four great border abbeys. Sir Walter Scott is buried here with his family. A giant statue of Wallace the patriot stands above the abbey, while not far away is Scott's View which was Sir Walter's favourite view of the Eildons over the Tweed.

'The Roman Road'

MELROSE—LAUDER

DISTANCE: 15½km (9½ miles)   HEIGHT RANGE: 85–285m

A not too strenuous walk, easily accomplished well inside a day and suitable for all types of parties. Several minor roads cross the route, allowing escape to lower ground in bad weather. Melrose, Lauder, and Earlston to the east of the Way, are on bus routes and have shops and a range of accommodation. A schooldays-only bus service calls at Earlston, Craigsford, Kedslie, Chapel Mains, Lauder, Blainslie, Bluecairn Cross, Langshaw and Melrose. A Border Courier service operates on Tuesdays, Wednesdays and Thursdays, connecting Lauder, Blainslie, Langshaw, and Galashiels.

From the centre of Melrose it is not far to join the Way on the south bank of the Tweed. Abbey Street runs north from the Market Square to the Abbey and Abbey Mill and to a road junction where you turn left to the Chain Bridge. Alternatively, you can follow the High Street from the Market Square north-west to the parish church. Steps down past the bowling green lead downstream past the weir which diverted river water to work the Abbey Mill and flush the drains. The Way goes east along the river for a short distance to the Chain Suspension Bridge – an early footbridge designed by J. S. Brown and erected in 1826. Byelaws prohibit horses, cattle and vehicles from crossing. Bicycles are not to be ridden and loitering, climbing, or intentional swinging of the bridge, is not allowed. Light carriages up to 3cwts may be taken across (by hand) under specified conditions. The penalty for contravention is £2 or imprisonment – the former presumably being the more welcome alternative in these days of inflation. Another notice states that no more than eight persons should be on the bridge

The Chain Suspension Bridge over the River Tweed

at one time whilst 'Passengers are requested not to cross the bridge in a heavy gale'.

Assuming that the weather does not prevent it, go through the Gothic stone pylon and cross the bridge on its wooden deck, with the massive iron link suspension chains supporting you as you bounce along. This is yet another splendid feature of the Southern Upland Way which those living in the south of Scotland take for granted, and those outwith the area seldom hear about.

Once across the bridge, the Way turns left to the west again along the north bank of the Tweed, ignoring the road running straight on to Gattonside. This village straddles the B6360 between Galashiels and Leaderfoot. The large villa of Allerly sitting slightly apart at the east end, was built by Sir David Brewster in the 1820s. Sir David was born in Jedburgh in 1781, trained for the ministry but became a pharmaceutical chemist, a lawyer, and a physicist – making his greatest contribution to the world in the field of optics. He invented the kaleidoscope and the holophotic system of lighthouse illumination and his achievements are commemorated by a cape in Greenland and a mountain in Antarctica, which bear

The Eildons from the 'Roman Road'

his name. He died in 1868 and is buried beside Melrose Abbey.

The Way skirts Gattonside by a very pleasant riverside footpath going west on the north bank. Both banks of the river here – back to Dryburgh, the Eildon Hills, and up the Leader Water almost to Earlston – are included as one of forty National Scenic Areas identified by the Countryside Commission for Scotland as areas deserving special protection. The north bank gives good views over the Chain Bridge to Melrose and up to the Eildons. Alders and willows fringe the riverside, which is subject to flooding at times, while beech and pine dominate the upper and drier banks. Mallard ducks are common and goosander and herons may be seen. Snowdrops make a bold sight early in the year, just where the path starts to climb from the river to the B6360. Care is needed for a short stretch on this narrow road as the Way follows it westwards round a bend to the brow of the hill. Then the road is crossed and a track taken straight uphill between hedges. The lane can be muddy but gains height quickly to leave civilisation below and return the walker to the uplands. There are expanding views to the west, to Galashiels

81

The Lauder Burn

sitting under the high mast at Langlee, and back over the Tweed to the twin peaks of Eildon North and Eildon Mid Hill.

The road to Gattonside Mains is crossed and the tarred road to the north followed for about 300m. Where the road bends to the left, leave it and take the track to the right. This passes between beech and hawthorn hedgerows with the beech having sprouted into quite sizeable trees now. The stone dykes met farther along this trail make an interesting comparison with their counterparts passed in Galloway. The smaller, flatter whin stones here are worked closely together in layers, forming a very compact and solid rampart. Here and there, bigger, squarer stones pattern the horizontal layering but it is the multitude of smaller rectangular stones, meticulously built into such a high dyke, that impresses one with the realisation of the labour involved. Capping the structure and contrasting markedly with the lower courses, is an overlapping shelf of miscellaneous boulders, each resting on its neighbour at an angle and giving a carefully designed impression of insecurity to deter man and beast from crossing.

The track forks right to Earlston and left and north to Lauder, with stiles marking the route ahead. A small burn is crossed and the track followed through a wood to a field. Enter the field and climb towards the pylons on the skyline, with the dyke close on your left and a rolling switchback of higher elevations on your right, rising to a neat little mount of trees. Notice the red earth in this farming country which ploughs into good arable land and grows green grass for pasturing sheep and cattle. Lauderdale is founded on Old Red Sandstone.

The view becomes more and more splendid as height is gained. The Scottish College of Textiles at Galashiels and the Galafoot road bridge over the Tweed stand out in the confluence of the valleys of the Gala Water and River Tweed. Above the two valleys stands the Minchmuir, bringing back memories for the eastward walker.

The electricity transmission lines carry 132,000 volts on the National Grid and 33,000 volts on the primary distribution lines. Pass right of Easter Housebyres, following the right side of the dyke, going north-east past the west end of a pond, heading towards woodlands. Left of the woods a remarkably straight road can be seen running across the landscape uphill and downdale. This is our Way, but to get there we first climb up through two gates to a small straggle of pines, crossing a dyke, and dropping down left of another dyke between a small loch on the left and a plantation on the right. This leads to a junction with a rough road from Easter Housebyres. Both routes join up now, heading northwards along this extraordinarily straight road which boldly ignores the contours and heads directly for the skyline over Kedslie Hill, crossing the road between Mosshouses and Cairneymount. Firm underfoot and straight as a ruler it has the hallmark of a Roman road and this is confirmed as we look back and find it heading straight from the Eildons.

The Romans under Agricola entered Scotland in AD80. Their advance was contested by the Novantae tribe in Galloway and the Selgovae in the Central Borders. As the Romans conquered or pacified the various tribes, they established networks of roads and forts to control the country and in AD142 constructed the Antonine Wall from the Clyde to the Forth, as a boundary between the north and the south. The advance of the Romans took place along Annandale in the west and by Lauderdale in the east. The eastern route over the Cheviots from York and Corbridge ran to Newstead and on by Lauderdale to Inveresk, Cramond and on up to Tayside. The Southern Upland part of this route is called Dere Street on today's maps, but between Melrose and

Lauder the route is lost!

Complicating the issue is another route called the Girthgate, which runs from Melrose to Soutra and is shown on Armstrong's map of 1771, and Roman camp sites near the Leader Water. Armstrong shows three routes north in this area. The question is – did the Romans make their road along a possibly marshy and forested river valley, or by a probably drier ridge where ambush was much less likely? The old road the Way is following is shown on Roy's map of 1747–55 running from Melrose to Lauder, but how old is it?

Those wishing to dispute the matter must walk the region first. It is undeniable that the Kedslie Hill route has an astonishing directness about it, characteristic of Roman boldness, and when its direction is so clearly aimed at the Eildon Hills it would be a remarkable coincidence if it were not deliberate. Anyone walking north from the Cheviots by Dere Street, or other ancient tracks such as the Wheel Causeway, will develop a similar respect for the early route-finders and their astonishing grasp of Scotland's geography. The Wheel Causeway runs under Bonchester Hill, straight for Ruberslaw and the Eildons. Once Dere Street has shaken off the Cheviots, there is no mistaking its destination either – the Eildons. Both routes treat these distinctive eminences like gigantic milestones along their courses, suggesting intelligent and organised thought on the part of their creators. Whoever continued the route over Kedslie Hill, heading for Chester Hill and its fort above Lauder, was displaying the same extraordinary skill in comprehending the landscape and going from A to B with the minimum of fuss. Modern man has lost this skill as he fumbles about in the valleys in his motor car and one of the joys of the Southern Upland Way is that it encourages us to rediscover the omniscient route, rather than assume that we know it already.

The Way is firm and straight over Kedslie Hill until a slight bend to the left takes us, remarkably, into softer walking conditions. Has the original route been lost hereabouts? This bend leads to a dip and then a climb past the farm of Bluecairn, where a conventicle was once held. A Covenanters' Well is shown on the map to the south-east of the farm. The Way joins a firm road again and passes left of the farm and its shelter-belt, to a cross-roads. It continues through this to the north, passing west of Jeaniefield. There are good views across the Leader Valley from here to the Lammermuirs. Continue by road to Fordswell. Here the walker leaves the road and enters a field on the left just short of a small plantation. A track is followed along the left edge of the field, past an Ordnance Survey trig point beside an overgrown quarry. Go under the electricity transmission lines to the north-west corner of the field, pass through two gates, and continue north-west on the west side of the dyke, up and down hill through pastures until a road is reached on Woodheads Hill. This is a public road from Lauder to Melrose. Cross it and continue left of a wood, along the edge of two linked fields, dropping down to a stile above the attractive valley of the Lauder Burn. Turn north beyond the stile and climb up again along a dog-leg boundary of wall and fence. Stay left of the fence and follow down the valley, well above a disused and fenced quarry, and below a wood bordering the Lauder Golf Course. Lauder is well into view now, though much of it is hidden by the ridge the Way is following. The earthworks of an ancient fort on Chester Hill lie at the end of the ridge but distinguishing the man-made fortifications from the man-made bunkers for the golf course is now a job for experts.

Between the wood and the fort the path slants downhill to the burn where there is a footbridge – but this should not be crossed. Stay on the east side of the burn with the path, crossing a lesser bridge. Notice the slopes above the far bank where the outlines of strip cultivation show up clearly. Farther down the burn, the path and Way cross another footbridge to the west bank to see similar patterns on the slopes of the east bank. These are the Burgh Acres, where the Burgesses toiled on small land divisions of a type common in Scotland before the days of intensive cultivation brought larger fields and modern methods. Lauder is unusual in still holding to these rights and customs. The Burn Mill is passed as the route steps on to the road from Melrose again – and this is followed into the town along the Mill Wynd to the right of the church.

Lauder Parish Church was built in 1673. It has a Greek cross plan with an octagonal bell tower and was designed by Sir William Bruce, who was employed at the nearby Thirlestane Castle by the Duke of Lauderdale. The predecessor to Bruce's church at Lauder stood near Thirlestane Farm, until its demolition. It was in Lauder in 1482 that the incident known as 'belling the cat' took place. In the face of an English invasion, James III was camped at Lauder, surrounded by his favourites. The Scots nobles jealously resented these 'low-born' courtiers but were afraid to act against them until one of them retold the fable of the mice holding a meeting to decide how to deal with their· enemy, the cat. The mice decided to tie a bell round the cat's neck to give warning of its coming – but a problem arose in finding a volunteer to do the tying. 'I will bell the cat,' said the

The 17th century Lauder Church with its octagonal bell tower

Earl of Angus, and, with the Earl as ringleader, six favourites
were seized and hanged over Lauder Bridge before the King's
eyes. The site of this Lauder Bridge is not known.

James Guthrie was minister at Lauder from 1638–49 and
was subsequently executed in Edinburgh in 1661 as the first
Covenanting martyr.

Beyond the church, the Way enters the centre of the former
royal burgh at the Tolbooth and turns right down the East
High Street. The Tolbooth has been burnt down and rebuilt a
number of times and it served as the town jail and council
chambers. The forestairs lead to the council chambers and
there is a bell tower with a clock. Lauder, in common with
other Border towns, has its annual Common Riding
ceremonies. The Tolbooth is the central point for the ride-
out, which is here accompanied part of the way by the
Lauderdale foxhounds. This is foxhunting territory and the
wrought iron name sign at the entry to the town incorporates a
fox in the design. The Black Bull Hotel in the Market Place
was a Georgian coaching inn, for this was an important stop
on the Edinburgh road. The railway to Fountainhall ran its
last scheduled passenger services in 1932 and today the town
is served by bus.

Lammermuir

LAUDER—LONGFORMACUS

DISTANCE: 24½km (15 miles)   HEIGHT RANGE: 180–445m

An experienced walker should find this a fast section, with good tracks for most of the route. Problems could arise in bad weather, though. The walk maintains a medium height over long areas, is lonely, exposed, and can be subject to mist and poor visibility, when navigation can be difficult. For these reasons it demands respect, particularly from the inexperienced. Anyone losing their bearings should beware of wandering northwards into the heart of the hills, when help lies to the south. Sheep ranching is carried out in the Lammermuirs with lambing on the lower ground, cattle grazing, grouse management, some forestry and water conservation for public supply. There is a good range of accommodation, services and bus routes at Lauder. Longformacus has a hotel, bed-and-breakfast accommodation, a shop and post-bus service to Duns on Tuesdays, Thursdays and Saturdays.

The Way leaves Lauder southwards on the A68. From the Tolbooth, the route passes along East High Street which becomes bounded on the left by the wall of Thirlestane Castle grounds. Before the last houses are reached on the right, the Way goes left into the castle policies, dropping downhill steeply past the stables with an interesting weather vane showing another fox. At the foot of the slope, the road runs on to the castle while a branch to the right leads to the exit from the grounds. The Way takes a track to the river, through a gate leading to a concrete bridge over the Leader Water.

Thirlestane Castle developed in three main stages. The grandly imposing western frontage which meets the visitor dates from the 17th and 19th century. The older 16th-century house runs to the rear to form a T-shape. This older castle is

Thirlestane Castle from across the Leader Water

remarkable in the number of circular towers jutting from its walls – four at the corners, with four smaller stair turrets in the angles, and two turrets and a central stair turret on each of the two long walls.

The Duke of Lauderdale employed Sir William Bruce to carry out alterations to the castle about 1670. These included the addition of the Great Terrace to the front and the dominating ogee roof, the flanking angle-pavilions and probably the remarkable parapet walk above the second floor of the old castle. Highly skilled royal plasterers were employed on the elaborate ceilings, while Robert Mylne was employed as mason contractor to Bruce before becoming a royal master mason. The wings on the west front were further extended in the 19th century by David Bryce. The red rubble of Bruce's work is warmer and lighter in tone than the darker whin used by Bryce. The Duke of Lauderdale was Prime Minister to Charles II and the 'L' from his name joins with four other initials to give the word 'cabal' which referred to a secret council of five ministers. The word originally derived from the Hebrew.

The ninety-eight-roomed castle is still lived in but is open to the public on various days, according to the season. Enquire locally for details. The Border Country Life Museum is a fascinating recent addition to the castle and there is a shop and tearoom.

Returning to the concrete bridge over the Leader Water, the Way turns left along the east bank, to an attractive but decaying iron bridge with a rose motif on the struts. Turn away from the river here, following a track which becomes a path up the left side of a field. Continue on this as it curls northwards between the fence and a plantation. A short section of forest road is walked, then the path taken again, still by the fence, ignoring tracks to the right until the path bends north-eastwards up the valley of the Earnscleuch Water, through birch woodlands, to clear the forest south-east of Drummond's Hall. Go south-eastwards now along the dyke, and up to join the A697 Carfraemill to Greenlaw road opposite the side road to Wanton Walls. Looking back from the road, Drummond's Hall is seen as being on the line of an old coaching road to Edinburgh from the south, which joins up with the more twisting A697 near Norton.

Take the tarred road uphill to Wanton Walls. A sign at the farm asks drivers not to exceed 7mph. This very precise but intelligent limit has been altered by a clandestine hand to 71mph – which is decidedly excessive for a right-angled bend through a farmyard! Walkers can take the bend comfortably at 3mph or so and follow the road uphill to the water board's white-painted pumping station. Pass this on the left and continue on a track through a field to a stile into the Park Hill Plantation, which is the southern extension of the Edgarhope Wood. Follow the track through the plantation and take the right branch where it splits. This leads downhill and out of the wood to the gap north-west of the neighbouring Bonnet Plantation. As soon as the plantation is left, turn sharply uphill again through the gap. Climb a stile and head across the field on the Park Hill side to another stile. The view south is impressive on this climb, to Lauderdale, Black Hill, the Eildons and the Cheviots.

The volcanic Black Hill, Earlston at its foot and Lauderdale, are associated with the legendary Thomas the Rhymer. Thomas of Erceldoune lived in the 13th century and was a poet and seer, with lands in Earlston. He has been styled the 'Father of Scottish Poetry' on the basis of his possible authorship of *Sir Tristrem*. According to Sir Walter Scott, Thomas was carried off to Elfland by the fairies and dwelt there for seven years before being allowed to return to the earth, returning later to his mistress, the Fairy Queen. The ruins of an old tower, standing near the Leader Water at

Earlston, are said to have been the abode of the Rhymer, while the parish church shows a stone inscribed 'Auld Rhymer's race lies in this place'. Sir Walter's house at Abbotsford is near the Rhymer's Glen, where Thomas is said to have met the Fairy Queen and departed for Elfland – the Eildons. These remarkable hills are also associated with the Arthurian legend, to the effect that an army of warriors lies sleeping in the hill, ready to rush to the defence of their country when needed.

The Leader Valley is one of the shortest routes to England from the eastern Central Lowlands. Through this gap have passed warriors, reivers, outlaws, vagabonds, minstrels and mountebanks. It is not really surprising that it should possess such a rich heritage of legend, folklore, ballad, semi-history and fact.

From the hill north of the Bonnet Plantation, the view opens out to the north and east. Ahead to the north stretches the long regular elevation of the Lammermuir Hills on the heathery horizon. Two remote little pimples at the right end signify the substantial summit cairns of Twin Law above a square-sided plantation. The shapely mound of Dirrington Great Law is farther to the right. The Lammermuir range is the final big barrier to the sea, so note these features well – as they will dominate your sights for the next few hours.

Leaving the far view for the time being, the walker drops down on a north-easterly course to the Snawdon Burn. Cross the burn between a grey shed and a pink shed and move from the right-hand side of the dyke to the left, and continue over the next rise. The raucous squawks of pheasants have been left behind in the woodlands now, replaced by the sounds of the wide-open spaces. The well-oiled, liquid triplets of the curlew, the resentful complaint of the lapwing, the modest chirp of the meadow pipit, and the prolonged ecstasy of the high-hovering skylark are all part of the pleasurable experience of these rolling agricultural lands on the edge of the Lammermuirs. This is sheep country again and care should be taken not to disturb flocks.

The Way heads down again to the Blythe Water, heading up the west side of its valley on a good track as the burn turns at right angles towards the south-east. This corner provides enjoyable views of the river, to where it has come from and to where it is going, with the Cheviot framed in a V-shaped gap. The opposite bank is steep and stony, lending character to the scene as it forces this tributary of the Leader Water to work its passage out of the hills in agile contortions. Much of the charm of the Lammermuirs lies in the intimate and hidden corners of these youthful river valleys. The lack of distinctive

The Standing Stone at Braidshawrig commemorating the 12th Earl of Lauderdale who was killed by lightning here

summits in the range can lead strangers to write off this area as scenically dull and monotonous. In doing so, they miss some surprisingly impressive features hidden in the folds of the hills – some of them unique in Scotland.

The old track continues up the west bank of the Blythe Water to Braidshawrig, but the Way leaves it nearly 1km (½ mile) from the right-angled bend and just downstream from the junction with the Wheel Burn. Cross the Blythe Water by a new bridge to the east bank, and slant up the ridge north-eastwards by a muddy track, to a gateway in a dyke with a stile beside. The old track is seen below, on the far bank, heading for Braidshawrig. It is one of a great number of variations of what is called the Herring Road. In olden days the monks and country people tramped these routes, bringing home a supply of salted herring from Dunbar to the abbeys and villages. The original Herring Road runs from Dunbar to Lauder but inhabitants from other areas made variations to suit themselves.

On gaining the crest of the ridge, the Way passes to the east side of the fence and follows this along the Scoured Rig. A tall, well-built cairn stands off to the right on the edge of the ridge. The fence leads to a road heading northwards into the rectangular plantation seen from far back. Follow the road, which splits the plantation in two, and emerge on the open hillside again looking down to Braidshawrig and the Blythe Water. Continue northwards down the slope on the road to the farm, bypassing it on its right by staying east of the water. A standing stone, just south-east of Braidshawrig between the dyke and the burn, marks the spot where the 12th Earl of Lauderdale was killed by lightning in 1884 while out grouse shooting.

Braidshawrig is empty now and has a barn, some sheds and some fairly big trees beside it. Tracks lead from the farm north and west to Sebastopol and Bermuda. Whoever bestowed these names must have been well-acquainted with the better-known originals of the Atlas. They could hardly be less appropriate for this lonely moor! The Blythe Water splits at Braidshawrig into the Wester Burn and the Easter Burn. The Way follows the road on the east bank of the Easter Burn and curls with it eastwards again as it climbs up through a line of grouse-shooting butts.

The relatively dry climate and the modest altitude of these spacious moors make this a good area for heather and red grouse. Grouse feed mainly on heather and the health of a moor determines the number of birds it can support. Along the next 4km (2 miles) or so, the walker has an opportunity to study grouse management – the rotational burning-off of the old heather, the ditching to discourage the formation of bog, the control of grazing by animals, and the construction or excavation of shooting butts from which the guns blaze away as the birds are driven over them by beaters. The shooting season starts on August 12th while heather burning (called 'muirburn' in Scotland) is permitted from October 1st-April 15th, or to April 30th in a wet spring. The heather is burnt in strips or squares to provide new young heather shoots as a source of food to the birds, while retaining some of the older, rougher heather as nesting sites. Grouse shooting, combined with sheep rearing, provides a viable commercial undertaking in this area. Walkers are requested to exercise caution and avoid causing disturbance during the shooting season and wait while drives take place.

The road from Braidshawrig climbs eastwards, then turns north-eastwards to the west of Nun Rig. Twin Law is now much nearer and the tall stone cairns crowning its summit take firmer shape, although the far one appears (falsely) to be lower than the other. The sheep steadings and barns dotting the moors are a surprising sight but, in the Lammermuirs, sheep graze to the summits and there are a number of farms not far off, hidden in the valleys. The firm state of the land-rover track is a great boon to walkers but it turns northwards

Twin Law Cairns

away from Twin Law at a barn beside a rather ragged-edged plantation. This plantation is a key feature on the route going in both directions, as there are few conspicuous features otherwise, to aid navigation. It is tempting to make directly for Twin Law across the moor but the depression along this line is boggy and time-wasting. It is better to stay with the road, which soon turns north-eastwards again at a shallow quarry, running upwards round the depression to stop at a fence running along the ridge. Rutherford's Cairn is conspicuous to the right on the southern side of the ridge. It is a well-built compact cairn of medium height.

The ridge and fence are followed south-eastwards to a Y-junction of fences and dyke. Cross the southerly fence into Berwickshire – the last one of the eight district authority areas crossed by the Way – and head south of east to the summit of Twin Law. In misty weather, the dyke on the left can be followed for about 1km (½ mile) then the high ground ascended to the south, or miss out the summit and continue eastwards with the dyke.

The summit of the hill is crowned by the Ordnance Survey trig. point and the two tall, barrel-shaped cairns which are so prominent from afar. These rise out of two large heaps of stones which may have been gathered together by early man as burial or ceremonial cairns. The present well-built, upright cylindrical towers atop the heaps are of comparatively recent date, having been built after excavation of the base cairns. Each has a southward-facing stone seat recess built into it, where a walker may take a sheltered rest – unless the wind be from the south. The western tower has a passageway cut through the surrounding heap of stones to a set of steps leading up to its seat. The eastern tower has a similar passageway, ending in a low recess under the tower, while a side channel leads to steps leading to the seat. There is a small quarry east of the summit where many of the stones were probably obtained.

A ballad called 'The Battle of Twinlaw' relates how a Scots and a Saxon army sent out their champions to do battle. The champions fought to the death, not knowing that they were brothers who had been parted in youth:

> 'And they biggit twa cairns on the heather
> They biggit them round and high
> And they stand on the Twinlaw hill
> Where they twa brithers lie.'

One version refers to them as sons of 'Auld Spotyswode' and another as sons of Edgar. There is an Edgar Burn rising near Twin Law, while the Way has already passed Edgarhope Wood. Spottiswoode House is south-west of Twin Law, near Westruther. In the transactions of the Berwickshire Naturalists Club Vol. 30, Lady John Scott of Spottiswoode is quoted, in reference to the two great cairns, as 'being shot down or overrun in 1944 by Polish tanks' and rebuilt.

The name Twin Law may well be a corruption of another name and the legend may have originated later as an attempt to fit an explanation to an improperly understood sound. Does Blackadder have anything to do with the family which included a Covenanting minister imprisoned on the Bass Rock – or is it a corruption of Black Water? Are Watch Water and Pulpit Law relics of Covenanting days? Or the Mutiny Stones – which have also been called the Meeting Stones? Was Rutherford's Cairn built for a shepherd or the Covenanter born at Crailing? One could speculate for ever on the names on the map. While there is no great tradition of support for the Covenanters in the Borders, the Duke of Lauderdale was an enthusiastic supporter up until the execution of Charles I.

The view from Twin Law looks south over the Merse of Berwickshire to the Cheviot. Astonishing formations of shelter-belts stand out in this landscape like ranks of armies drawn up for battle. Green, yellow and brown fields pattern the plain, while the Eildons dominate the south-west as usual, with Black Hill and Ruberslaw to the left. The Manor and Moorfoot hills present a high but monotonous line to the west, then farther right the Pentlands break over the mid-distance, pretending to be bens in the Highland zone. Higher Lammermuirs block the view to the north, patched and scarred with the annual ritual of muirburn. Even the summit of Twin Law has seen the firestick. What a sight it must have been to see these weird towers girdled with fire like Brunhilda's punishment rock.

The Watch Water Reservoir to the north-east is a welcome sight in this lochless region. Streams and rivers still dissect the land in all directions but the Eastern Borders are Sahara-like when you search for expanses of standing water. However, the eastward-bound travellers are not likely to be over-concerned at this stage with finding lochs in the landscape. They are more likely to be searching the horizon for the North Sea – and finding it from Twin Law if the visibility is reasonable.

To the right of the Watch Water Reservoir stand the two shapely peaks of Dirrington Great Law and Dirrington Little Law. The Way descends towards the reservoir, giving a view between these laws to the North Sea and Lindisfarne – the Holy Island off the north-east coast of England. The descent down the east ridge is easy in mist if a course is taken north from the summit for several hundred metres to the dyke running west to east across the hill. The dyke has to be crossed to the north side, anyway, and you will find the necessary stile where another dyke joins it from the south some distance down the ridge. Then a fence continues down, leading south of Twinlaw Wood to join a track and turn north along it across a footbridge beside a ford on the Watch Water. A memorial stone sits above a well on the north side of the ford. The inscription is very worn but bears the dates 1865–97 and relates to a keeper at Rawburn. It is inscribed 'There is no water on Lammermuir sweeter than of John Dippie Well'. A sandstone exposure on the river bank gapes a red scar in this green setting, where snipe and oystercatchers make their home by the river.

The track being followed runs from Wedderlie to Dye Cottage but is left by a north-eastern branch to pass the farm of Scarlaw among its trees, and join the tarred road beyond. The road follows a shelf above the Watch Water Reservoir and gives a good sight of the Dirrington Laws across the water. The foundations of an ancient peel tower are passed near four trees, then the road becomes public to vehicles at the spillweir beside the dam. Fishers and picnickers frequent the route now. This is a public water supply and visitors should take care to safeguard the purity of the water. The Way follows the road beneath the dam and round the side of the reservoir. The sandstone outlet tower bears the legend 'B.C.C.1954' – Berwick County Council then being the local authority involved. A pink granite stone has been used to face the wall along the top of the dam. This makes an unusual blend with the red sandstone and the grass sown on the slope.

The road and the Way climb steeply away from the reservoir, through shooting butts, giving a fine view back to Scarlaw. It is unusual to see butts so close to a public road. If the birds only knew how to sit on a car bumper they could hitch a lift past the shooting cordon with impunity. Rawburn Farm sits high on the other side of the hill and the road takes a long descent from here past the waterworks sandwiched in a peninsula between the Watch Water and the Cross Burn. The water treatment plant bears a 1954 datestone and sits above slurry ponds just before the road crosses the Watch Water and passes into a wooded glen rich with bird-life. Rathburne Hotel on the left is very conveniently situated for walkers, then the burn is crossed again just before it joins the Dye Water. Past the confluence of the two rivers there is a weir which was constructed to channel a flow into a lade above the far bank for Longformacus Mill downstream. You can compare the levels of the lade and river as you walk downstream on the road, passing a huge quarry and playing fields, to the bridge linking the two halves of Longformacus.

The single-arch stone bridge has an elaborate stone tablet facing downstream, though it is hard to see this properly. Two stone heads are built into the wall at its north end, along with initials and an 1851 date. There are some attractive Georgian buildings in the village. The older part is grouped about the river, with more modern expansions up the hill to the north. Some of the older houses have been modernised, others are in the process of being renovated, and original stonework, harled and pebble-dashed walls, stand side by side.

The church is up a drive on the south side of the river, facing the Way-walker entering from the west. A notice proclaims it as 'Longformacus Parish Church founded 1243'. The present building dates from the end of the 19th century and looks quite small from the drive. When seen from the cemetery it appears very much larger. It has a rounded apse at the east end, and some of the stones in the churchyard date back to the 18th century. Up the hill to the south of the bridge, the trees almost hide another part of the village, including the only shop and the post office. East-bound walkers, now only 27km (17 miles) from the end of their coast-to-coast odyssey, might imagine they can already smell the salty tang of the North Sea!

Whiteadder Water from Abbey Hill (outer)

Whiteadder

LONGFORMACUS—ABBEY ST BATHANS

DISTANCE: 12km (7½ miles)   HEIGHT RANGE: 145–310m

The walker now has a short but very interesting section ahead, with frequent changes of scenery to maintain the interest. Some alertness is called for in map-reading as it is easy to forget about these direction changes and find yourself off the route. Camping is not allowed on Abbey St Bathans estate but rest-house type accommodation is being provided by the estate in the village. A post-bus operates between Duns and Abbey St Bathans every Monday, Wednesday and Friday. A school bus runs between Abbey St Bathans and Duns during the school term. However, vacant seats cannot be guaranteed.

The route continues from the bridge on the Dye Water in the middle of Longformacus and follows the road uphill to the south-east towards Duns. At the top of the village, the Way takes the minor road to the left, along the edge of South Bank Wood. Views of the church and Longformacus House (which is attributed to William Adam's design) are glimpsed through the trees. Caldra Farm is passed and the road dips to cross Blacksmill Burn. On the far side of the burn a stile crosses the fence on the right hand side of the road. With a fence on your right, follow the edge of the field, turning uphill to another stile leading onto hill ground. Keep north of the plantation and the smooth strip of pasture replaced by the Gas Board after pipe-laying. The track crosses the foundations of an old settlement, where the grass-covered stones make odd-looking humps and depressions beside the smooth ground to the south.

Under the power cables and over the top of the hill, a new landscape is revealed of commercial forestry and amenity planting at Whitchester estate on the left, contrasting with treeless moors to the right. The correct route is east, on a mean between the two, moving from grass to heather to pass over the Sel Burn and through a gap left of a red barn and an isolated thicket. Avoid straying to the north towards the first shelter-belts of beech trees. Once the Sel Burn is crossed in the dip, the route continues east, going well uphill with shelter-belts of beech on both sides now. Follow round the right-hand edge of a field to the derelict shepherd's cottage of Commonside. This is in a lofty position and may be seen from far off unless a heavy summer foliage of beech masks it until you are almost upon it. The building is now an unofficial dovecote and a flock of wood pigeons is liable to explode from it when anyone approaches its extensive, nettle-bedded precincts.

A few metres higher on the ridge, the Way turns left along the edge of the field. Backwards down the slope lie the wooded valleys of the Dye and Watch waters. Longformacus House is seen in the open, Rawburn is prominent on its hill-top and Scarlaw looks a long way back through a gap. Twin Law's cairns are growing insignificant but Dirrington Great Law is still a great peak on the landscape, as it has been for some time. The land is becoming much more intensively used than farther west. The big hills are all to the west now and the mean height of the landscape is lowering. This is reflected in more fields, greener scenery, more livestock, and earlier lambing.

Eastwards lies the depression of the Whiteadder Water, with steam rising from the mills on the valley floor. An old footpath goes south from here over Blackhill to Langtonlees and Polwarth while the Way goes in the opposite direction.

Keeping the fence on your right, continue north-eastwards up the ridge past two gates and round the right-hand edge of a field at the edge of a belt of trees. The valley of the Whiteadder makes an impressive gap in the landscape to the north while the big house at Whitchester is seen to the north-west at the hub of its estate. The Way is approaching this estate now – downhill through fields on a rough tractor track towards a funnel-mouth of trees. This leads into the Lodge Wood and down the forest road on to the B6355 Ellemford Bridge to Duns road. Turn left along the road, past Whitchester Lodge. Those going west turn into the plantation by a gate immediately past the lodge and once out of the trees, head south-east for the skyline.

The lodge is in Scottish Baronial style with coats of arms, initials and 1897 dates in stone and on the tall iron gates. The grounds are open occasionally under the Scotland's Gardens Scheme. The road twists down to a dip where the Way leaves it again, turning sharply off to the right, following a rough road steeply uphill along the top of a plantation. Keep above this plantation, contouring around the western slopes of the hill, and take your reward in a splendid view up the Whiteadder Valley. The scenery is neither rugged nor dramatic – but it has a special quality. Like much of the charm of the Southern Uplands, it has to be experienced to be understood and appreciated. There is a cinemascope breadth to the landscape, spreading upwards from the glinting, curling river to its adjoining green flats, its raised terraces, the farms and patchwork fields, shelter-belts and plantations, to the great curving sweeps of the heather hills on the horizon. Through it runs the road to Cranshaws and up into the Lammermuirs, with the promise of steep gradients and an exciting journey ahead for those who would win along this highway. On the left, the minor road from Ellemford Bridge rises to Rigfoot and goes on and on rising, until you are looking up to Whitchester. The convex slopes of this landscape are restful to the eye and mind, understating the hilliness of the area. There are no great heights here but it is far from being a flat area – as walkers will have discovered. The North Sea could be a hundred miles away at this moment, for all the walker can sense of it.

Walkers will be there before the river though. The Southern Upland Way follows a south-west to north-east course and is nearly across the Uplands now. The Whiteadder is generally flowing along a north-west to south-east course out of these Uplands, with the coast running away from it until the Tweed is joined, many miles on, near Berwick.

At the moment, river and Way travel together, the latter following a dry track through the heather along the ridge above the river valley. The next objective is a forest road through Roughside Wood running along the flank of Abbey Hill (outer). The forest can be recognised by the stripes of different trees species planted under the dome-shaped summit. Darker green pines and spruce contrast with the lighter greens or browns of the larches. Before this forest can be reached, a tributary burn chops a gash into the hillside in front of the walker, called the Robbers Cleuch. The track is forced eastwards around the top end of the near forest to descend steeply to burn-level and enter the forest where a road makes a U-bend over the burn.

Follow this forest road northwards with trees on either side of you. Temporary diversions may be in force in this area when forestry operations are being undertaken.

At first there are few glimpses of the river, but after the valley bends to the east, more and more gaps in the trees

Welsh Black Cattle in the valley of the Whiteadder Water

afford wonderful views of the valley, with a spectacular vista at the end as the road descends out of the forest to a meadow opposite Barnside. The views up-river are very attractive, too. Continue along the road at river level past Mountjoy Wood and into the open, with the valley of the Monynut Water coming in on the left. Welsh Black cattle are prominent in this area. The Shanno Herd is said to be the largest herd of Welsh Blacks outside Wales. Pedigree fell ponies are also bred on the estate and may be looked for about Abbey Hill. The rough road wends its way through the fields, to drop right of Abbey House into Abbey St Bathans opposite the church.

According to tradition, there was a religious settlement here in the Dark Ages. Then, around the end of the 12th century, a Cistercian priory of twelve nuns and a prioress was established. The remains of the priory have been incorporated into the parish church, which was given its present form in the mid-19th century. A stone effigy of a prioress lies in a recess inside the church. It was found among the earlier stone work when the church was being remodelled. There is no evidence of an abbey ever being here. The village probably got its name at some time from someone's uninformed knowledge of religious orders. However the mistake arose, it certainly caught on for there is now an Abbey St Bathans House, an Abbey House and two Abbey Hills!

The churchyard has some interesting memorials dating back to the 18th century. Opposite the churchyard is an estate building which is being converted into a rest house for use on the Way. The turreted Abbey St Bathans House is seen to the south-east from the church and, if the road is followed past the house, the entrance to the trout farm, interpretive centre, tearoom and picnic area is soon reached. These are open to visitors from 11.00 to 17.00 daily until the end of September, and on Saturdays and Sundays from October to May. The Centre has an attractive display of nine murals by Susan Millard, depicting life in the valley from the Bronze Age to the present day. These include the boat ferry, which once took worshippers to church across the Whiteadder before a bridge was built, the 18th-century Retreat House, Abbey St Bathans House in its former days as a cottage, the priory, and Edinshall Broch – which is the major tourist attraction in the district. Brochs are unique to Scotland, being tall, wide, circular dry-stone towers without windows. They are associated with the Picts and are numerous in the north of Scotland, but rare in the south. Edinshall is an eminently large example, although little of its height remains.

Across the Whiteadder from the trout farm, the Weir Burn – as it is known locally – or Whare Burn, according to the OS map, enters the main river. A bridge crosses the Whiteadder to reach this valley on one of several attractive walks being provided by the estate.

Abbey St. Bathans over the Whiteadder Water

Pease Burn

ABBEY ST BATHANS—
COCKBURNSPATH

DISTANCE: 16½km (10 miles)   HEIGHT RANGE: 0–230m

A pleasant and varied section to end (or begin!) with, providing something for everyone, from the expansive clifftop panorama to woodlands and rural lanes. Roads are never far away, so no walker should be in trouble on the route although the cliff section should be treated with respect. The busy A1 has to be crossed, where fast-moving traffic has to be allowed for, but if walkers show patience there will be no accidents. The major part of the route goes through farming areas with some forestry. Cockburnspath has a range of services and accommodation for walkers and is on a bus route to the Central Lowlands and England. There are also shops at Cove, Pease Bay and Grantshouse and the latter has some accommodation. The nearest youth hostel is at Coldingham which is on a direct bus route. The post-bus from Duns calls at Grantshouse, Bowshiel, Blackburn Mill and Abbey St Bathans every Monday, Wednesday and Friday.

The final section of the walk leaves Abbey St Bathans from the church to cross the Whiteadder Water. The old footbridge opposite the church is unsafe and is to be replaced, while the path through the woods on the opposite bank has also deteriorated to a dangerous state above steep drops to the deep river. Until this route is open again, walkers should follow the road north-west across the Whiteadder by the bowstring girder road bridge, and on over the Monynut Water, before turning back uphill past Shannobank.

Much of the charm of these picturesque valleys is due to the indigenous oakwoods which have survived here, clinging to the sides of the valleys where the slopes were too steep for cultivation. Amenity planting below them in the mid-19th century has added attractive variations, in the colour and

105

shape of copper beech, gean, cypress and other species.

The Whiteadder is now a big river and is met here about half-way along its course from its source on Dunbar Common to its junction with the Tweed in England. Several of the source burns rise very near the edge of the Lammermuir escarpment and have little work to do to eat their way back over the edge and flow in the opposite direction to the Lothian plain.

Once above the junction of the Whiteadder and Monynut Waters, the track from Shannobank is taken north-east over the hill. It has the appearance of a drove road, with its rough surface and enclosing boundary dyke and fence. Roy's map of 1747–55 shows a road from Shannobank to Blackburn. The track drops to the Whare Burn, turning left upstream at a wooden barn to cross at a bridge and ford. There are numerous rabbit warrens along the burn which maintain a small local industry in the provision of rabbit meat for export.

Climb straight out from the burn on the other side, going over a stile and under electric power lines to cross pastures to a cairn, crowned by a red-painted rooster weather vane. It is said to have been erected by a Mr Cockburn, the former occupant of Whiteburn Farm, to celebrate the 100th anniversary of his family's connection with the farm. This field can be muddy and it comes as a relief to join the hard concrete lane past barns and shelter-belts at the north end. With the rising ground, the views improve again, to Monynut Edge in the north-west, the main Lammermuirs in the west, the Whiteadder Valley to the south, and Hardens Hill with its aerial – which was seen by east-bound walkers from Commonside not so long before.

The lane crosses the public road, passing left of Whiteburn Farm and by a track straight on into the fields. Extra stiles have been provided at the fences so that walkers can choose the left or right side to walk, depending upon the current crop rotation. Choose the field that is in pasture to avoid trampling crops. Follow the edges of the fields north and then north-east to join the public road on Quixwood Moor. Turn left along the road and, at the end of a wood on the right, turn right downhill on a farm track to Blackburn, which is seen high across the valley. The Eye Water is crossed in the dip near the site of an old cornmill and a bend in the track taken before climbing the now-metalled farm road to the big farm of Blackburn, with its extensive array of barns, byres, pens and cottages. Some of the older buildings carry red pantiles on their roofs – a typical east-coast building tradition. Pass right of the two-storey houses, farm buildings and a new bungalow and follow the road as it curves down to join the A1 at

Shannobank and the valley of the Monynut Water

Bowshiel Wood. The Pease Burn is in the valley on the left now leading you, at long last, to the sea. 'Valley' is too weak a word in the Lammermuirs. The Pease Burn is out of sight below in Bowshiel Dean. A dean is a steep-sided glen in this area. Yet again on our Uplands traverse, we meet a new word, honed for a special topographical meaning. Bowshiel Farm on the far slope shows a tall chimney. There are a number of these attached to farms in Berwickshire, generally dating from the 19th century and used in combination with a boiler and engine house.

Turn left on the verge of the A1 trunk road, being careful of the speeding traffic on this main east-coast road between London and Edinburgh. Those turning off it going west will find Blackburn signposted at the road-end. Those heading for the east coast follow the road northwards, crossing it when it is safe, and following a section of the old road between the new road and the railway. Road and railway were re-routed slightly to the west in 1979 when the Penmanshiel Tunnel collapsed on the railway.

The North British Railway opened its line from Edinburgh to Berwick in 1846. The rivers Tweed and Tyne were

An Inter City 125 train above Pease Dean

formidable obstacles to the completion of the east-coast route from London and, for a time, passengers were bussed between Newcastle and Berwick. The completion of the Royal Border Bridge at Berwick in 1850 allowed through trains to run from London to Edinburgh and the north. The first express trains between London and Edinburgh took 12½ hours for the journey. Today, the Inter City 125s do the journey in under 5 hours. The introduction of the new international-sized freight containers on to British Rail's network required modifications on this line in 1979. The 130-year-old brick-lined Penmanshiel Tunnel was too small to take the 8½-feet containers safely, so while one line remained in use, the other was lifted and the ground scraped away to lower the track. It was while this work was in progress that the 256m-long tunnel collapsed, burying two workers. Because of the looseness of the rock, and the danger to the rescuers, attempts to bring out the bodies were halted. The ground was consecrated, and a new gap gouged out of the hillside to take the present line. A plaque on the hillside commemorates the two men.

From the Blackburn road-end, it is about 1km (½ mile) north along the side of the A1 to a bridge across the railway, and the entry on the far side of the bridge left into the Penmanshiel Wood. The Way follows the forest track northwards, parallel to the railway, skirting to the left of Penmanshiel Cottage. Emerging from mixed woodland into an area of newly-planted conifers, the track joins another forestry road. At this junction, take a sharp hairpin bend to the right, followed shortly by another to the left, climbing steadily to gain views of the Pease Dean below, the railway, the A1 – and the sea!

The Fife coast and the new nuclear power station under construction at Torness are the advance signs for the coastal landscapes imminent in the final wind-up of the walk. Broom and whin are colourful by the track at its highest point beyond Broad Wood and as it descends by Aikieside Wood. Both plants are bright yellow but broom is the brighter, with bigger flowers, while whin (or gorse or furze as it is also called) has sharp spines. The Inter City 125s speeding past on the railway have a distinguishing yellow colour also which is carried well back on the loco cabs, giving them the nick-name – flying bananas.

This walk through Pease Dean is an attractive and interesting experience, partly due to the natural history – it is particularly rich in butterflies and birds – and partly due to the grandstand view of the outside world, including the A1 and the railway. Robert the Bruce was in Pease Glen in 1317, preparing for a siege of Berwick, when a letter was delivered to him from the Pope. He sent it back unopened as it was not addressed correctly to him as King of Scotland.

The woods lead to the A1107 Cockburnspath to Coldingham road, just east of Pease Bridge. West-bound walkers should take the upper of two tracks through the woods beyond the second gate. Pease Bridge seems a fairly ordinary bridge from the Way, so it is well worth an extra 100m walk on to it to appreciate its true quality. It was built in 1783 and the parapet is 36m above the burn. At that time it was thought to be the highest stone-built bridge in Europe, if not the world.

Traffic flows so swiftly along the A1 and railway today that it is easy to overlook the communications problems posed to the early travellers. The main route to Scotland was once inland through Lauderdale. As for the earliest east-coast route, walkers will shortly see its hazards for themselves. Pease Dean was a fearsome alternative. During the 'Rough Wooing' in the 16th century, when the Duke of Somerset invaded Scotland, a chronicler reported 'so steepe be these bankes on eyther syde, and depe to the bottom, that who goeth straight doune shall be in daunger in tumbling, and the commer up so sure of puffyng and payne'. It was partly due to military pressure that the 1783 bridge was built. At one time a number of forts straddled the Pease Burn, controlling this valley. The bridge is of red sandstone with four arches, a middle pier rising from the bottom of the gorge, and two shorter piers from the sides of the gorge. The designer was David Henderson of Edinburgh who incorporated pierced spandrels in the structure to lighten its load. The bridge has iron railings on top of low parapets, on which, unusually, are two OS bench marks.

Sessile oak is the predominant tree in the gorge, with ash and elm colonising the better soils, while sycamores are common alongside the track through the woods. Those wishing to escape from the walk are now on a bus route (A1107). Just across the A1 is Tower Farm above the remains of Cockburnspath Tower. An earthwork fort looks down on the scene from Ewieside Hill above the glen.

The Way crosses the A1107 and joins the Forestry Commission's Pease Dean Forest Walk which drops down to Pease Bay on the east side of the Pease Burn. This goes through pleasant and varied habitats, with the sea beyond lulling the walker into a false sense of completion. As the glen flattens out you pass the site of Pease Mill. Two paths meet here and the west-bound walker should take the left one. The east-bound (now north-bound) walker crosses the burn and comes out on a road near the entrance to the caravan park, which has a seasonal shop.

Follow the road left as it climbs steeply up to Old Linhead. A building here was once an inn, with stables for trace horses, used in pulling stage coaches up from Pease Bay. This was the Edinburgh to London coaching road before the building of Pease Bridge. The Way turns right just before the first building at Old Linhead, and leaves the minor road for a path across a depression and the Cockburnspath Burn to the cliff edge. The burn is in a very small hanging valley from which it cascades in a waterfall to Pease Bay. The views are superb from the cliff although the caravan park could be much-enhanced with some tree-planting. Below is the sandy beach with two burns trailing into the sea. Sandstone was once quarried near the mouth of the Pease Burn. Then the ground rises to the ruin of the Norman Church of St Helen, sitting in a drainage channel cut by glacial melt water diverted southwards by the Scandinavian Ice Sheet moving west across the North Sea. Siccar Point to the left was the scene in the 18th century of James Hutton's important discovery of

Cove Harbour and the tunnel through the sandstone cliff

Looking east to Fast Castle Head from above Cove Harbour

the unconformity of the rocks here, with the gently inclined Old Red and Carboniferous Sandstone beds supported on the upturned edges of the Silurian. With the evidence before him of sedimentary rocks of different ages, and the folding and contortions that have taken place, he propounded his theories which are the foundations of modern geology.

The headland on the extreme left is Fast Castle Head, where the fragmentary ruins of Fast Castle date back to the 15th century and are said to have suggested the Wolf's Crag to Sir Walter Scott for his novel *The Bride of Lammermoor*. The cliffs running beyond it round the corner rise 100m and are among the highest sea cliffs on Britain's east coast. There are very few harbours on this exposed coastline but St Abbs and Eyemouth are well worth a visit. Eyemouth has a museum and a long memory of the storm of 1881 when its fishing fleet was destroyed and 129 men lost.

This cliff walk is airy and exhilarating but needs care, good footwear and good footwork. The slopes are grassy and angled rather than rocky and precipitous, but for that reason they need special caution in several places as the dangers are less obvious than on sheer rock. With sensible footwear and feet firmly planted flat on each step an unhurried progress will carry anyone safely across the steeper parts. Careless or hurried steps invite trouble, and should be methodically avoided. Holidaymakers from the caravan site take this route regularly so it should not cause any problems to sensible walkers.

The route is channelled safely between two fences at first. Stay out of the fields which lie on the inland side, but keep close to this fence to avoid the steep ground falling to the shore. In places the route is broad and well away from all danger, with foundations for war-time buildings, and a hard surfaced track to follow.

The cliff line is followed left for about 1km (½ mile), passing above Cove Harbour to the edge of the cluster of houses at the road end at Cove. The views are well worth a two hundred-mile journey – notwithstanding the twin-chimneyed cement works and twin-reactored Torness power station. Barns Ness Lighthouse, North Berwick Law, the Bass Rock and the Isle of May set off Fife and beyond in the background, while the indented crag-line of the Berwickshire coast is nearer at hand.

Cove Harbour is a very impresssive spot, with a hard rib of sandstone to the north sheltering a sea-filled hollow washed out from the softer coals, shales and limestones. Two angle-bent piers have been built out to shelter this inlet, with 18th-century cottages (now serving as stores) on the edge of the inclined access road. On the opposite side of the harbour, tucked under the cliffs, is a trim private dwelling which was formerly used for smoking the fish. Access to this dwelling and the sandy shore is by a 50m-long tunnel bored through the sandstone rib. House martins frequent the red headland above the tunnel, while fulmars and gulls have colonised the steeper cliffs beyond the harbour. Borders Regional Council now administer the harbour, which is used by several lobster boats at all states of the tide, finding a narrow channel through the reefs from the east.

The tunnel is a most unusual and interesting feature and dates from the 1750s. It has recently been renovated by the council and is worth traversing for the dramatic experience. It can be reached by following the harbour road from the car-park at Cove village. The Way on the cliff-top path and the road converge near this car-park. The village has a coastguard station and a shop. Cars are not allowed down the harbour road. The view is impressive from the edge of the village, along the vertical cliff to Reed Point and down to the lines of undercut and inclined skerries which break up the heaving sea into white water. Eider ducks bob upon the swell, manoeuvring deftly among the currents.

The Way turns south on the east side of the first houses reached at Cove, and climbs inland again for its final kilometre. It follows a path between two hedges, passing west of Cove Farm and its five-arched carthouse, by the left of two descending tracks. A road is crossed and a track taken left of a row of dwellings to a high arched underpass beneath the east coast railway line again.

Cockburnspath is now visible across a field, and all that remains to be done is to follow the track to a house on the A1, turn left to the war memorial and enter the village by the road right of the hotel. A bend to the left reveals the village square and the thistle-crowned mercat cross which is the official end – or start – of the Southern Upland Way. Near it is the entrance to the parish church. This is a long, narrow building with a slated roof and a stone slab-roofed burial aisle at the east end. It has a most extraordinary flat-topped round tower at the west end. The churchyard contains a number of elaborately carved memorials which are worth inspecting at a leisurely pace as the Way-walker winds down from the great trek. The village contains the hotel, passed on the route in, toilets, two general shops, a shoe shop and cobbler, a doctor's surgery and – for one hour a week – a sub-branch of the Royal Bank of Scotland.

Long-distance walkers will react in different ways to the completion of their 340km (212 miles) coast-to-coast trek

The mercat cross at Cockburnspath—the eastern end of the Way

across Scotland. Some will gratefully accept a seat on the steps of the ancient mercat cross, while they take in the knowledge that their labours are over. Some may adjourn to the hotel to celebrate – and some will scan the notice board near the post box for the departure time of the next bus. Some walkers may retrace their steps to Cove or Pease Glen, for a more leisurely inspection of these scenic splendours, or move on to explore Duns, Eyemouth, St Abbs Head and other attractions in the area. The insatiable could always tackle the Pennine or West Highland Ways on their road home, or join those walkers just starting out for Portpatrick! However they react, and no matter how fresh – or exhausted – they feel, none can rob them of the distinction of having completed one of Britain's finest long walks.

Appendix I

SELECT BIBLIOGRAPHY

Fact or Fiction?

In describing the rich heritage of the Southern Uplands in this Guide, an attempt has been made to distil the culture of centuries from a wide variety of sources. Legend, folklore and propaganda are all bound into a people's culture, along with documented fact. It can be extremely difficult to disentangle one from the other – even when official papers are consulted. This guide has sought to steer a careful course through this minefield, qualifying its statements with cautionary scepticism where a tale is worth telling, though its source may be elusive. To ignore the unsubstantiated legend completely is as foolish as to accept official documents uncritically. The lines of study suggested by a traverse of the Southern Upland Way are so rich and diverse that no student could possibly exhaust them in a lifetime's research. The books listed below may, however, provide a starting point for the enthusiast.

The Southern Uplands (East): Beattock to Cockburnspath

British Association for the Advancement of Science (1951). *Scientific Survey of South Eastern Scotland.*

Cameron, Alex. *By Yarrow's Stream.* Albyn Press, Edinburgh.

Clavering, Molly (1953). *From the Border Hills.* Nelson.

Curle, James (1911). *A Roman Frontier Post and Its People.* James Maclehose & Sons.

Grant, Will (1948). *Tweeddale.* Oliver & Boyd.

Hardie, P. R. (1942). *The Roads of Medieval Lauderdale.* Oliver & Boyd.

Johnston, G. (1853). *The Natural History of the Eastern Borders.*

Rankin, Eric (1981). *Cockburnspath, a documentary social history of a border parish.* T. & T. Clark, Edinburgh.

Scott, Sir Walter (1803). *The Minstrelsy of the Scottish Border*, 3 vols.

Thomas, J. (1969). *The North British Railway: Vol. I*. David
& Charles.
Thomson, A. (1880). *Lauder and Lauderdale*.
White, John Talbot (1973). *The Scottish Border and North-
umberland*. Eyre Methuen, London.

One of the biographies of Sir Walter Scott and of James Hogg
could be read for a better understanding of the importance of
these writers in the Borders.

General

Andrew, K. M. and Thrippleton, A. A. (1972). *The Southern
Uplands*. Scottish Mountaineering Trust.
Edlin, Herbert L. (1969). *Forests of Central and Southern
Scotland*. HMSO.
Feachem, Richard (1977). *Guide to Prehistoric Scotland*.
Batsford Ltd.
Geikie, Archibald (1901). *The Scenery of Scotland*. Macmillan
& Co.
Glasgow Archaeological Journal, Vol. 4 – *Studies in Roman
Archaeology* (1976).
Haldane, A. R. B. (1971). *The Drove Roads of Scotland*.
Edinburgh University Press.
Manley, Gordon (1975). *Climate and the British Scene*.
Collins.
Margery, I. D. *Roman Roads in Britain*.
Millman, R. N. (1975). *The Making of the Scottish Landscape*.
Batsford Ltd.
Moir, D. G. (1975). *Scottish Hill Tracks: Old Highways and
Drove Roads. (I) Southern Scotland*. Bartholomew &
Son Ltd.
Murray, J. and Pullar, L. (1910). *Bathymetrical Survey of the
Scottish Freshwater Lochs*, Vols 1–2.
Natural Environment Research Council (IGS) (1971). *British
Regional Geology: The South of Scotland*. HMSO.
Pearsall, W. H. (1968). *Mountains and Moorlands*. Collins.
Scissons, J. B. (1967). *The Evolution of Scotland's Scenery*.
Oliver & Boyd.
Stamp, L. Dudley (1969). *Britain's Structure and Scenery*.
Collins.
Thomas, J. (1971). *A Regional History of the Railways of Great
Britain: Vol. 6 Scotland – The Lowland and the Borders*.
David & Charles.
Weir, Tom (1972). *The Scottish Lochs 2*. Constable.

Readers are also reminded of the inventories of ancient monuments, transactions of the local history societies, the county histories, and the various editions of the Statistical Accounts for the counties of Wigtown, Kirkcudbright, Dumfries, Lanark, Selkirk, Peebles, Roxburgh and Berwick, as sources of further information.

Scottish Long-Distance Footpaths

Aitken, Robert (1984). *The West Highland Way* (revised edition). HMSO.

Andrew, Ken (1984). *The Southern Upland Way*. Vol. I (West). HMSO.

Appendix II
ACKNOWLEDGEMENTS

The Southern Upland Way is the end product of a great amount of thought, discussion, documentation and hard physical work, involving many people with a wide range of talents. The Countryside Commission for Scotland has worked closely with landowners, farmers and foresters along the whole length of the Way, with the local authorities in southern and central Scotland, the Forestry Commission and other statutory bodies; with units of the army, the Scottish Conservation Projects Volunteers, and numerous individuals. The author of this guide wishes to pay tribute to the many people involved in devising and creating this fine route. As a latecomer to the team, the author has not had the time or opportunity to meet all of those concerned with the project, and he may never know all their names.

I would like to thank the librarians, foresters, landowners and others who have helped me personally. It is impossible to single out individuals for credit, but, without them all, the Southern Upland Way – and this guide – would have remained ideas rather than becoming realities.

Ken Andrew
Prestwick 1983

Government Bookshops
13a Castle Street, Edinburgh EH2 3AR
49 High Holborn, London WC1V 6HB
Brazennose Street, Manchester M60 8AS
Southey House, Wine Street, Bristol BS1 2BQ
258 Broad Street, Birmingham B1 2HE
80 Chichester Street, Belfast BT1 4JY

Government publications are also available through booksellers

The waymark symbol used by the Countryside Commission
for Scotland for long-distance footpaths in Scotland

Published for the Countryside Commission for Scotland by
Her Majesty's Stationery Office, Edinburgh

Countryside Commission for Scotland
Battleby, Redgorton
Perth PH1 3EW

Printed in Scotland for Her Majesty's Stationery Office by
Bell and Bain Ltd., Glasgow